SIDE HUSTLE IDEAS

CRUSHING IT WITH PASSIVE INCOME USING YOUR
LAPTOP TO WORK FROM HOME AND MAKE
MONEY LIKE A MILLIONAIRE

SHELDON LEONARD

"Everybody says they're trying to get their piece of the pie. They don't realize that the world is a kitchen – you can make your own pie."

— TERRY CREWS

SIDE HUSTLE IDEAS

CONTENTS

INTRODUCTION

Congratulations on downloading *Side Hustle Ideas: Crushing It with Passive Income Using Your Laptop to Work from Home and Make Money Like a Millionaire* and thank you for doing so.

The following chapters will discuss what passive income is and how you can get the most out of time by doing high-value money activities. When it comes to creating a passive income stream, there are a lot of things to consider, and this book will get into details about every aspect needed to take conscious and smart investing decisions.

This book will provide you with amazing strategies, that have allowed people to make a lot of money and become financially free. It will also give you a complete overview of the most famous concept that every online marketer should learn: how to properly delegate activities to make the most money.

The goal of the book is to speed up your education and save you time and money along the way.

Before getting started, it is important to note something about mindset. This, like the other books in the series, will not offer "get rich quick solutions," since they do not exist. Especially when you are beginning your journey in creating an online business, it is fundamental to focus on learning and acquiring new information, rather than just chasing money. With the right knowledge, results will come much faster, and you will be amazed by what you can accomplish, even with a small capital. The book wants to give you the tools you need to get started and share with you some of the golden nuggets that made other people wealthy. If you study this material carefully and start applying it, you will lay out the foundation for prosperity and wealth.

There are lots of books on this subject on the market, so thanks for choosing this one! Every effort was made to ensure it is full of as much useful information as possible. Please enjoy!

1

THE RIGHT MINDSET

Before we begin, it is imperative to comprehend something about mindset. Most people seeking passive income try to get there with a passive mentality. Bad mistake. It's the fastest road to failure. To create an autopilot business, you need to be pro-active and take the bull by the horns. Here are seven tips you need to know before getting started.

1. 'Passive income' is viral

You can do what you love most and get paid for it. That's the dream. To the bank teller, the journalist, or the hustler who spends all day struggling with clients, this idea is a dream. Drop everything. Devote yourself to your passion. Let the money show up by itself. It's viral, alright. Otherwise, one couldn't explain why people get hooked on the idea so quickly and easily, after only a few courses or webinars.

2. Is it possible to create passive streams of income?

Yes, in my opinion as long as you work hard for 4 or 5 years to learn your specific area of expertise, how to organize work in a certain way and how to monetize your clients the most, it is definitely possible. The point to understand here is that it takes a lot of time and perseverance. And no, one month is not a lot of time.

3. Ok, I understand: you want to leave a job that you do not like, create passive income and dedicate yourself to the one you love the most.

But then excuse me, since you have to spend 4 or 5 years to study how to create passive income and then dedicate yourself to what you love, why do you not spend that time trying to figure out how to turn what you love most in a job?

What I advise you to do is: do what you want, and turn it into a job. It takes certain character to do it, but we must also know how to do it. It's one of the ideas you will hear about the most in the self-development niche.

4. The 'pure' passive income does not exist.

Unless you make a great marriage or win the lottery - even managing the system that gives you money 'automatically' takes time and effort. I have friends who do network marketing. With this idea of creating their passive income they have more meetings than the CEO of Burger King, they meet a lot of potential customers to create their own network. And you want to tell me that it is not hard work? Do you think that the network should not be nourished after it is created?

5. Choose something that you like so much that you do not even think about it as a job. This will greatly facilitate the creation of a true passive income.

I know people who wanted to create their passive income by doing stock trading (one of the things I am an expert in – I have written multiple books about this topic). They are the most stressed people I know in the world, by dint of being behind systems, numbers and everything else that work entails. Would you be able to manage it?

When you will have your passive income (you decide how much), what do you want to dedicate yourself to? It's worth spending some time trying to answer this question - Probably the key to your professional evolution is here. It's something that people never think about. They spend their lives thinking that first, they have to do something to earn money and then dedicate themselves to something they really love to do. From a logical point of view, it is nonsense. Yet choosing what you love and trying to make it the center of your work seems to be the hardest thing in the world.

6. Creating a passive income is always a 'process,' not an ending act, and to follow this process, you must learn to anticipate the change that takes place in the system.

Years ago, one of the most effective systems to generate 'almost passive' income was to open an automatic videotape rental business. Today there are no more automatic videotape rental stores, and I have not seen one for at least 10 years. How many systems today can generate a passive income and are able to sustain this capacity over time? This is an important question to ask yourself if you want to be in this game for the long term.

7. Creating 'passive income' is possible only if you are willing to change your mindset and the way you operate.

The way you decide to organize yourself, your job, and that of your collaborators to bring the whole system into a position where it has a very strong sense of identity - and operates from there.

When all the people in the organization align 'who they are' to what they do - the whole structure becomes more efficient by several orders of magnitude. And only then, in my opinion, it is possible to start thinking about generating passive income.

Hands up those who have never dreamed, even if only for a moment, about a life based on economic independence and financial freedom, where there's no need to work because the money comes from passive income streams, which only require monitoring and occasional 'adjustments' to keep them alive.

In order to live on passive income, however, it is necessary to have available a starting capital which, invested in an intelligent manner, is able to produce precisely the income that is necessary for you to live and which can also cope with the process of inflation, that as you know is not controllable by individuals.

I will not spend words to explain how much money you need to live on passive income, nor will I give advice on investment methods or real estate, since they are not my responsibility, but I will try to advise you some sources of passive income that will allow you to create an online automatic income that does not require special investments if not your intelligence, your experience and your time.

Of course, stop here and do not continue reading if you are not willing to make an effort to find that famous balance between income and expenses mentioned earlier, and if it makes you sick if you commit to a project that will only allow you to earn 50 or 100 euro per month online (one of many, of course, because it is a replicable mechanism, as we will see shortly).

I do not know how many of you like to travel and visit new places, personally as a digital nomad, the possibility of going to Spain, England and the rest of the world by continuing to manage my online activities from anywhere in the world is an aspect that I feel is particularly fascinating.

Of course, it is not something that I have always done, even though for most of my first fifty years of life I have worked mainly as a freelancer, so independently and being able to manage in full freedom the rhythms and working time (provided you deliver work on time, of course). But for some time, I have also worked as a 'subordinate,' commuting or working at night, enduring the uprisings in the middle of winter and uncomfortable train journeys, taking on extraordinary and exhausting shifts and everything that employee life can offer. All this, or having experienced the two sides of the coin, convinced me to do everything (including some sacrifice) just to conquer and keep the freedom deriving from freelance work and a passive income lifestyle.

The real breakthrough, however, was that of passive income, derived mainly from working on the Web and at online projects.

But what is passive income? In general, it is considered money earned without moving a finger or even while sleeping (it is not an exaggeration, as you will see shortly). Beware, however, because the so-called passive income is never completely passive, or at least not risky if you do not, at least sometimes, do something to 'support' the sources from which the streams derive. In fact, while doing so, you have the opportunity to feed the sources of passive income and to grow them.

However, it is right to immediately clarify a fundamental point, and underline again what was said at the beginning of this chapter: to create passive income without necessarily investing money you can rely only on your intelligence, your tenacity, your experience (the famous know-how) and on your time. You must, therefore, have all these resources available and use them together to create a model of automatic and passive income on the Internet.

In everyday life, the so-called "offline life," most of the work activities require active physical presence. This means that, in order to make money, you have to go to work every single day for a determined number of hours. If you are new to the concept of passive income, you might not have understood the issue with this just yet. Let me explain.

One of the limitations of "real" life is represented by the fact that, regardless of how much money can be earned at the end of the month, if you divide the profit by the hours that have actually been dedicated to that purpose, the final result will be a finite number.

Not a big deal, right? Well, not really. If you dig a bit deeper, you quickly realize that this means that the amount you can earn is limited, no matter how much you make per hour of work. Why? Because there are only so many hours that can be dedicated to working, which by default limits the total income that can be generated on a regular job. This is where entrepreneurship and this book come into play.

You see, if you decide to make money online, things change because you can make a profit from the comfort of your own home, even when you are sleeping. Wait, making money while sleeping? Yes, you read that right. Having an online business means having an asset, that can generate profits no matter if you are working on it or not. This is a crazy opportunity that you should take advantage of.

Thanks to the internet, we are now able to conduct regular and ordinary action in a matter of seconds. Just think, for example, that the web allows you to make investments, transfers, bank transfers, phone top-ups, view bank statements and much more with simple clicks. All this until a few years ago was not possible.

We mentioned that with an offline activity the earnings are "finite". It means that if, for example, in one month you work 160 hours and you earn 1,600 dollars then, technically, you have earned 10 dollars per hour, which is a finite value.

Suppose, at the same time, you also have an online activity that makes you 600 dollars a month automatically. You have actually earned that specific amount, with zero hours of actual work. This means that you have earned an infinite number of dollars per hour. Interesting, right?

It is clear that much of the work must be done in the initial part, to create the "system" that will allow you to earn money. But after that, the work is almost automated. Therefore, the revenues that you could obtain from your online business are of an order of magnitude far higher than that of classic work activities. The most interesting aspect of working with the web is that there is no limit to the number of activities you can start at the same time, nor are there any specific limits on how much each activity can make you. Obviously, to get profits thanks to the web is not easy, you need to have winning ideas and a minimum of technical skills. If you want to make money sustainably, then you will have to build an online business that provides the end customer with an added value over your competitors.

One of the problems that I see when I talk about passive income and the possibility to leverage the internet to generate recurring profits is that people try to get passive income using a passive mentality. This does not work and is the straightest road to failure. Just think passive income is like a skyrocket; at first, it requires a lot of energy to get up from the ground, but once it is in the air, there is very little energy that has to be spent on keeping this condition. When you are building an online business, it is important to understand that there is some work required, sometimes a lot of work to be more precise, but that ultimately it will pay off.

I understand that most people do not have a lot of time to dedicate on a business, especially if they have never been entrepreneurs before and are used to put in a limited amount of time per day. Well, with passive income and online businesses, it is fundamental to be committed, because the possibilities to give up are everywhere you look. Luckily enough, you do not have to reinvent the wheel, and you can live off what other people have discovered and tried before. In particular, certain business models work better than others.

The goal of the next chapters is to describe the processes that helped me generate more profit than my previous job (which I quit) did and that I know for a fact is replicable for anybody. Furthermore, I will show you the exact models I have followed to create streams of income that are sustainable and require little to no maintenance.

One final note of motivation before getting our hands dirty and really start digging deeper into this amazing world. I really encourage you to select one of the methods and stick to it until you are successful, before moving on to the other one at the first sign of failure. Each and every one of the techniques and business models described work wonders. You just have to go through the learning curve to see great results. Do not be affected by the "shiny object syndrome," which is the tendency to jump from one good opportunity to the other, without taking full advantage of it. I know you can do this because I did it as well. So, do not give up, keep studying and experimenting, put in the time and I am sure you will become one of those success stories that are out there.

Let's dive deeper and discover what are the best business models to create passive income streams.

In addition, you will have to work towards specific objectives and focusing on them, avoiding to disperse yourself in a thousand things and focusing only on what really matters to achieve the results you have set. In short, you will have to apply the famous 80/20 rule. What is it? Let's see in the next chapter.

THE PARETO PRINCIPLE

HAVE YOU EVER HEARD OF THE 80/20 RULE? SOMETIMES THEY CALL it the principle of the scarcity of factors, and it was originally called the Pareto Principle. It was born at the beginning of the 20th century when Vilfredo Pareto discovered that in Italy 80 percent of the land was owned by 20 percent of the population.

Fast forward a few years, we realized how the rule could be applied in the business world. In most cases, 20 percent of the customers represent the vast majority, or 80 percent, of their turnover. And today the 80/20 rule lends itself to any kind of interesting interpretation.

To take advantage of the 80/20 rule within your company, you focus on 20 percent of the best customers, which guarantee you 80 percent of your sales.

To take advantage of the 80/20 rule to manage your time you focus on 20 percent of the things you do, the ones that matter to you or your business. In other words, the highest value activities (also called "high money value activities").

Pareto's law is dramatically effective when applied to sales and marketing situations. However, the use of Pareto's theory in sales and marketing is generally neglected.

The Pareto rule at the simple level suggests that, if there are two groups of data typically related to cause and effect, or input and output, the correlation measured by the data of reality is that:

- 80 percent of the output is produced by 20 percent of the inputs.
- 80 percent of the results are given by 20 percent of the causes.
- 20% of the nature of the costs generates 80% in absolute value of the costs.
- 20% of customers generate 80% of revenues.
- 20% of products generate 80% of revenues.
- 20% of non-compliance causes 80% of non-compliance.

You can apply this relationship to any kind of variable. The Pareto principle is extremely useful, with infinite applications. Often the optimal ratio in terms of identifying the minimum percentage that will produce the best improvement is closer to 90:10 or even 99: 1.

The numbers in their ratio must not necessarily reach 100. The two numbers in an optimal ratio can have more than 100 or less than 100.

For example, there may be a situation where 99% of the result is produced by 15% of the factors or when 75% of the results are derived from 5% of the factors.

So even if a situation contains an 80:20 correlation, other relation ships may be more significant, for example:

- 99:22 (which demonstrates an even greater concentration of 80:20)

- 5:50 (i.e. 5% of the results comes from 50% of inputs or causes) which means a huge amount of activities with ineffective content).

The reasons that allowed the 80:20 ratio to become the "standard" relationship is that on large numbers it remains the most surprising and commonly found relationship in reality.

Remember, for any particular situation the precise ratio can and will probably be different from 80:20, but the principle still applies, and in many cases, the actual ratio will not be far from the general rule of 80:20.

This principle is extremely useful for planning, analyzing and solving problems and achieving goals.

Many disasters in the business could have been easily avoided with a consistent approach of the Pareto Principle. It is a tremendously powerful model, and it is so powerful because it is so simple and easy.

For example, consider an organization that continues to run its business across its product range, when perhaps 95% of its profits come from just 10% of the products and / or perhaps only 2% of its profits comes from 60%, the same with reference to customers.

Imagine the wasted effort. Instead, by making a quick analysis of "Pareto's rule" by discovering this reality, decision-makers can clearly see where to direct their efforts, and probably reduce a lot of bad products and better focus on customers and products that are more profitable.

THE BASICS OF PASSIVE INCOME

WHEN YOU LOOK FOR "PASSIVE INCOME STREAMS" ON THE INTERNET, you will discover that there are hundreds, if not thousands, of "strategies" that can generate profits on autopilot. From drop-shipping to Kindle publishing, from Amazon FBA to day trading, there are endless solutions to your financial problems.

However, one thing that I found out by working one on one with my clients is that all this information causes more confusion than clarity. Why? The answer is simple: because most of the people that approach an online business for the first time in their life have never created a business before. In fact, recent researches show that 83% of people trying to make money online come from a poor and financially uneducated background. This is a huge problem because it does not allow people to see things for what they actually are. For instance, one thing that most beginner online entrepreneurs have in common is the fact that they think that passive income streams consist of "technique, loopholes, and strategies that take advantage of a system to generate revenues." This could not be further from the truth, but I see where they are coming from.

The big issue that this mindset creates is that things are not approached professionally and the money quest is not considered as a real business. To put things into perspective, I have decided to make a clear distinction of all the methods that there are to make money passively. Before going through the list, please keep in mind that any other method you have heard of before falls into one of the following categories, so it should not be considered something else. By getting this distinction clear from the start, you will be set up for success. While in this chapter we showcase the 6 ways that passive income can be achieved, in the following chapters we are going to explore one method per category, so that you have a solid base and tangible and practical information to work with. Here is the list.

- Financial returns - Build a well-made portfolio of financial stocks such as shares, ETFs, funds, bonds, etc., and harvest the fruits year after year or month after month. If you do not consume the capital but, instead, let it grow by taking only a portion of the income, the game can theoretically last forever and produce true wealth. In some cases, this can be very simple as well, totally automated, relatively risky but, at the same time, extremely profitable as in the case of cryptocurrency investing, which I will cover in the next chapter.
- Real estate income – By keeping things simple, it is relatively easy to produce an income stream that goes on autopilot and brings in money every single month. One particular aspect of real estate that I have found profitable is the famous buy to rent, which I will discuss later on in the book.
- Copyrights and trademarks - Write a book, write a song (or limit yourself to writing the lyrics or composing the music), invent, or perfect something useful and while

someone else commits to selling it for you, you perceive a part of the profit as long as the public is still interested in buying it, listening to it or using it. A perfect example of this category is the so-called "white labeling," which I will explain later on in great details.

- Royalties - Similar to copyrights but in reality what you do is give up the use of something of yours to third parties in exchange for a fixed monthly amount or a part of the profits that come from it. For instance, the book you are reading or listening to right now is part of a passive income business that revolves around self-publishing.

- Unmanaged Businesses - Purchase a business that works (or, better still, a part of a business that works), and while your members or your employees or managers are committed to making it work, you limit yourself to perceiving a part of the profits generated by the same activity. A great example of this type of businesses can be found on flippa.com, and I will show you how to take advantage of them to create a passive income stream.

- High-margin products or services that generate recurring revenue - Software, subscriptions, maintenance, consumables, internet business, membership (and many other ideas that would be too long to list at the moment) are all ideas that belong to this category. Many times, it is a matter of transforming the sale of a one-off product into a recurring sale or a service. When I do coaching sessions with students about this particular category, I always mention the business model of drop-shipping, since it is one of the most famous.

Now that you have understood better that there are only 6 categories of passive income and that they are not loopholes or shady tactics, it is time to dive deeper and analyze each one and see how you can bring it to life. My advice is always the same: select one of the methods and stick to it until you get results.

Different passive income ONLINE business models

Now it is time to take a look at the different business models you can use to make passive income from your laptop.

1. Sell one or more services, automating the process as much as possible.
2. Sell content, in the form of books, eBooks, courses or info-products.
3. Sell through others, earning from affiliation.
4. Monetize content published in other ways (e.g., with advertising space).

At the moment I (like many others here in America and in the rest of the world) earn from all 4 sources. Naturally, each of these ways of creating passive income presupposes the initial work and, in many cases, also the subsequent work although sporadic to maintain the vitality of the source of income. As you have noticed, in fact, in all three cases we talk about "selling", which presupposes that there are buyers and that there is a need to reach them by letting them know in some way (possibly without investing in advertising), and at the same time that there is a "product" to sell to these people, something that may interest them for any reason.

We will try to examine these four ways one by one so that you can understand which one is the best one for you, that is, with which you feel more affinity in relation to your interests, your passions, and your abilities.

1. Passive income from the sale of services or online applications

This is one of the most effective methods to create an automated passive online income, but unlike the other three methods presented below it requires a small investment to register a suitable domain and Web space, as well as greater technical expertise.

For this type of passive income, in fact, we consider services such as ad sites or those that allow you to manage technical aspects of activity on the Web, proposed in the freemium formula, or with a free basic version that involves limitations of use and a more complete paid version where the limitations are 'unlocked'.

In the first category there are, for example, sites where people can post ads of various kinds made with themes or dedicated plugins (using CMS as WordPress), such as those for the sale of used equipment or to meet other people (ad sites) or online dating, or tourist portals that give visibility to advertisers and earn every time they sell their service (it is the case of the hospitality industry with sites like TripAdvisor, Wimdu, etc.), or other sites that put freelancers with potential customers in connection, and so on.

In the second category, on the other hand, there may be included sites that manage, for example, the backup of a site or its maintenance, facilitate networking or collaborative activities of a professional nature, and so on. It goes without saying that it is not enough to develop and put online this type of services, but that we must then promote them both initially and periodically so that more and more people are registered, and naturally we must manage them with an equally regular maintenance to avoid problems of stability or security on the site that provides them.

In addition to the sites, there may also be true applications, both in the form of computer software (desktop PC) and mobile devices (smartphones and tablets) in the form of an app. In this case, the skills required for their development are even greater, and once again there will be a need for promotion to make them known and updated over time to correct any stability and security bugs or improve their functionality making them even more attractive. Of this second sector are, of course, also the games, often proposed with a freemium formula and distributed as an app or inserted into websites (e.g., in gambling or multi-user games) or on social networks. Probably those who read will have already had the opportunity to play some of these games, or to take advantage of some services like those listed above.

At this point, it will be clearer what we mean when we say that there is no totally passive income, a concept that we will find even later, and it is, therefore, important to underline.

2. Passive income from the sale of contents

When we talk about content, we refer not only to those that form an eBook or a book, but also to images that a photographer can sell on sites specialized in stock images, or to video and to the audio sold in the same way. In all these cases, passive income streams will derive from the repeated sale of each individual content, which may produce a proper revenue if it is conducted on its own or partial if sold through a distribution platform. The latter are represented, for example, by traditional bookstores or those online in the case of books and eBooks, from the already mentioned sites that sell images (photos and drawings), video or audio for professional purposes such as the development of sites or multimedia products, or again from sites that host, for example, online courses if the contents already mentioned represent a video course or an audio course.

In all these cases, the content must be produced only once and then placed on the market through an automated sales system, and this is how the flow of passive income is created resulting from its sale. As can be understood, even for content, promotion and marketing are essential if we want to increase sales rather than simply wait for someone to notice them and buy them (something that happens), and for those contents that are subject to obsolescence (for example, courses on technical subjects) it is also necessary to proceed with periodic updates so that they remain attractive to the public and do not become too old (and therefore no longer valid) because someone decides to buy them again.

A strategy often used by those who live from the production of content is to offer a fragment for free, for example through a site or a blog, and create parallel commercial versions that collect them as a book/ebook, full course, and so on. In this way it becomes possible to create a 'showcase' able to support the commercially distributed 'works,' and thus increase sales.

3. Passive income from affiliate marketing

If you don't want to sell your services, products or content, you can always do it with those of others by earning a percentage of those sales and thus creating another form of passive income. In this case, however, the sale takes place outside of your site, directly on that of the seller. In America, the opportunities for affiliation are many and offer ample earning space.

Passive affiliate streams of income can also derive from sources other than a website. For example, it can be from content published on social networks. However, in this case they have a shorter duration in time and it becomes less likely that the public will notice them and click on the respective links (unless you periodically invest in paid visibility, as you do for example on Facebook. Highlighting the payment of a post, in this case, we will fall into passive generated by a cash investment, however minimal, so it is not appropriate to include it in this chapter. Do not worry, we will talk about passive streams of income that require a monetary investment in the next chapter.

4. Passive returns from other monetization of contents

The latter category may include, for example, services such as the sale, or rather the rental of advertising space on a site or app that enjoys a certain popularity/visibility. The advertising spaces can be represented by text in a directory, by banners or entire pages, as it happens for example in the sites/portals that are positioned in the tourism sector and rent space to managers of hotels, restaurants, and similar activities inside of strategic areas of the site. This is more valid than ever in such a field, given that advertisers will be more likely to pay their periodic share the more they are certain of gaining visibility through the site.

The same applies to the apps, once they have achieved the necessary popularity, but the latter typically require investments in marketing and advertising to gain visibility among the public.

This type of passive income should not be confused with income generated through systems such as those used by portals like TripAdvisor, obviously, as in this case, it is an automated service and therefore falls into the first type of online passive income described in this chapter.

4

20 IDEAS TO MAKE MONEY WITH YOUR LAPTOP

I PUT TOGETHER THIS SHORT LIST OF QUICK IDEAS TO GET YOUR MIND working and thinking about the types of things you can do to get started making money with your laptop. Here are 20 simple ideas to get your juices flowing.

Social trading

Would you like to enter the investment world and earn as much as a professional trader but you do not have the skills?

We are talking about online trading and therefore buying and reselling financial securities but in a much less technical and decidedly more humane and "simplified" way.

With social trading, your portfolio will copy the investments of the Popular Investors you have decided to follow. If they earn, you earn accordingly.

Flipping comic books

Do you have a passion for comic books, or did you have it in the past and without knowing you find yourself in the cellar a discreet little treasure?

Well, I have good news for you: the comic book market is enjoying a happy time, reaching a turnover of 200 million euros in America.

In this context, deciding to start a comic flipping business could turn out to be a truly profitable business. And doing so through Catawiki, an online auction portal with 12 million visitors a month could be the winning choice.

Become a social media manager

Do you have a passion for the world of social networks? Monetize, otherwise you're just wasting time and money.

Exactly, you can earn with your ability to manage social profiles, in fact, companies will be happy to pay you to be their voice on social networks.

Become a data enter

This is not a business idea, but you can create extra income in your free time by answering the most varied surveys. Companies need to gather the most information from their customers and potential customers, so they create market surveys and also need your opinion.

Many sites offer paid surveys with cash or gift certificates, all belonging to international market research companies.

Become a graphic designer

Are you a creative person who loves the computer world?

Becoming a graphic designer would open up a professional world in which you could express yourself as a freelancer. But to be attractive to companies and be able to stand out from the crowd you need to study hard, so be prepared for it.

Become a copywriter

In the last 15 years, with the advent of the web, big publishing portals, and online stores, were born.

All these entities are related to the world of writing but do not necessarily have a journalistic/editorial career behind them. If you like writing this is a great second online job.

Create and sell t-shirts

If you are an artist looking for a way to get people to know you, why not create T-shirts with your ideas?

Draw, paint or print your sketches on simple t-shirts. You can resell them online and make a profit.

Create an app

Nowadays the applications for smartphones and tablets are endless, but if you have noticed a gap in the market and you have a winning idea, go all in. Some websites help to implement them, step by step. The marketplaces of the main IT brands help to sell them, holding 30% of the profit. There are different procedures, so it is good to see the regulations of individual companies.

Sell books

Surely you will have at home some books you have read and which you are not interested in keeping anymore. Take advantage of them, you can sell them, to partially recover the expenses you had. The used book market has some success, especially in this day and age.

Become a software tester

If you know English, some companies propose to test computer software and give rewards for it. The tester is chosen on the basis of specific criteria from time to time, according to the needs of the program, so be ready to receive a few "no," before finding a task.

Sell your photos

Do you have a passion for selfies or photographs? In addition to keeping them on your smartphone or posting them on social networks, you can publish them on portals that sell them for about 10 euros. You earn money based on downloads.

Start a blog

To work as a blogger, it is good to be creative, but sometimes it is not enough; being a blogger also requires a minimum of knowledge of social networks and the main web marketing strategies.

The work of the blogger starts from the creation of a blog, but having a blog does not necessarily imply a profit, it's undoubtedly a springboard to be known, propose services, spread your opinions and also become an influencer, which you can then leverage to make money.

Become an SEO expert

SEO activity is part of the professions that allow a very high online profit if you are good: the SEO specialist deals exclusively with search engine optimization of all those rules that allow you to optimize a blog or a website to ensure an increase in traffic coming from search engines. Big companies spend a lot of money every year one SEO.

Open an e-commerce

Opening an online store to sell your products is a relatively simple operation, if you know how to do it: now more and more people buy online, more and more sites are optimized for mobile devices, for this reason, if you have an activity and you want to earn money online with an e-commerce you have to be present on the web and sell your products in an online store.

Earn by sharing links

Yes, it is possible to earn from home also by sharing links: it seems strange because the "like and share" is now becoming the activity that we all do naturally. Anyway, some companies pay to share links of news, articles, events, post that refer to their website in order to increase visits.

Make money with YouTube

Making money with YouTube today is definitely a very common and popular way to make money on the internet: the "YouTubers" today are just real people who shoot videos and earn by posting them on YouTube thanks to the spread of the videos that become viral.

Post reviews

We have already seen how the surveys allow you to earn a little bit, but you can also get money online through reviews of products and services.

For example, you can earn by posting reviews of books, hotels and tourist sites to get cash or prizes or discount coupons.

Online betting

Online betting is another effective method of earning on the web especially for those who are passionate about sports: most web-based bets concern games or sports events and obviously require a certain skill and study in order to understand and achieve results. Today some portals or bookmakers issue bonuses for the first registration, so it is convenient to subscribe to more online platforms to have more possibilities for betting and earning.

Become a consultant

Many professionals rely on the web to earn online and offering services via the web. This is the case of the field of web marketing, where the competition of the agencies is ruthless, and the experts in marketing activities juggle with the tools in their possession to get commissions and jobs. Becoming a consultant in this field is extremely good to make a full-time income online.

Become an online translator

Even translators and teachers often rely on the web to make money. Through ads or personal websites, but also using portals for professionals like Linkedin, you can earn online thanks to the sharing of your skills.

5

BUY TO RENT – SIDE HUSTLE IDEA #1

THE ACTIVITY OF A REAL ESTATE INVESTOR IS OFTEN misunderstood. Most people, when hearing the term "real estate investor" think, "ok, this job earns a lot of money, it is fun, it is easy to do, and it is all sunshine and rainbows," but the reality is not like that. At all.

This information that is disseminated all around the internet is not correct. The activity carried out by a real estate investor is a methodical activity, it is an activity that takes a long time to master. The investors have to do a lot of visits to real estates; they need to make a lot of proposals knowing that most of these offers will be rejected, as you can imagine.

It is important to operate with a large number of real estate visits and proposals to obtain results. In other words, the idea that the real estate investor walks and makes money is absolutely false; it is a very difficult job.

What I would like to tell you is that this is an extraordinary profession, where you can obtain very important personal and economic satisfaction, but it is necessary to work hard before resting on a sustainable passive income stream. It is necessary to have a lot of time, and it is necessary to know from the beginning that it will not be easy. If you could automatically earn, everybody would do it, which is absolutely not real, we know it very well. To do something and get a result you need to commit, so if you are interested in the world of real estate investments, you must know that it is a difficult job like all other investments. It is a job where you'll have to spend time, where most of the answers you receive will be "no." You will not have to give up, you'll have to continue and if you manage to be consistent and do things the right way you will be able to clearly get results not only at the economic level but also at the level of personal satisfaction.

Here are some (for most people) shocking truth about investing in real estate.

Your dream house is not an investment, did you know that?

The property owned, or the house of our dreams - or villa depends on the possibilities of each of us, has always been considered a sacred "asset" in America. A goal to be achieved as soon as possible at the cost of any sacrifice. And indeed, we are the people with the highest percentage of homeowners. About 80% of Americans own a home. It does not matter if we take out mortgages for thirty years (sometimes even longer) with monstrous installments that most often absorb around 50% of the income of an average family. The important thing is to "own" our home. Good, this is what smart people do, right? False. Almost nobody that is rich lives in a place he owns. As Grant Cardone says, "rent where you live and own what you can rent."

The question I want to ask you now is this: do you think buying a house is equivalent to buying an asset or a liability? The answer is clear and not debatable. Among the mortgage payment, various charges, government, and municipal taxes, when buying a house, you buy a liability.

But we better explain the concept of liability. By liability, we mean everything that generates cash outflow from our family income statement. By contrast, by asset, we mean everything that generates positive cash flow. For example, I buy an obligation that usually brings a coupon, this coupon represents an income, and therefore the obligation is an asset.

The sad truth of the American real estate market

But how strange: we make so many sacrifices to buy a house, yet we buy a liability? Yes, dear readers, in America, unfortunately, the investment property is almost completely unknown. In fact, there is no real estate market in the true sense of the word. And for the real estate market I mean the sale of an asset, in this case, the house, in order to realize a capital gain and therefore an investment income. Trades usually in America in the vast majority of cases are made because a couple decides to get married and then buy a house, or move after the coming of children, etc. In summary, following a family necessity and not for investing, as usually happens for financial or business investments

The ventures of real estate investing

But at this point, the question to be asked is this: is it possible to transform the purchase of a house from a liability into an asset and consequently obtain a monthly income or make a capital gain? Well, dear readers, the answer is fortunately yes! Not only is it possible, but it is desirable that each of us in the investment process of our assets dedicate part of the capital to real estate investments.

Real estate investing has some notable advantages, for example, it is possible to receive monthly income (rents) and at the same time realize capital gains at the time of sale. Precisely because of the characteristics of the market in consideration, such as the American one, the investment in real estate, in fact, is a more than secure investment, as the value has been pretty stable over many years.

At the beginning of this book, I mentioned that I really like the "buy to rent" model. This means buying a property and renting it out, collecting revenues every single month like clockwork. Why do I like it so much? Because it gives me a predictable stream of passive income, something that everyone should aspire to. But how does this work? Here it is.

The winning formula

Let's hypothesize to buy a house of $200,000 with a minimum investment of $40,000 (but some banks also finance 100% of the amount) and that with the rent we cover only the mortgage payment. Well, after 10 years assuming an average revaluation of 4%, our house has been revalued for a value of around $296,000, which means that $40,000 has become $96,000 in 10 years. In practice, an annual profit of 14%. Not bad, I would say, especially if compared to the yields of bonds and some liquidity/money funds that fill the wallets of American savers.

At this point you may ask, "after 10 years we sell the house, right?". Wrong. Once the mortgage has been paid off, it is when the fun starts. Now, in fact, you have a stream of income that brings in money every single month and goes on autopilot, whether you are thinking about it or not. Your goal, if you decide to go down the real estate investing world, is to accumulate as many properties as possible, so that in a no distant future, you will have your living expenses covered by the different rents. This, in my opinion, is passive income at its finest.

6

CRYPTOCURRENCY INVESTING – SIDE HUSTLE IDEA #2

THE SECOND STRATEGY THAT I AM GOING TO EXPLAIN TO YOU IS investing and, in particular, investing in cryptocurrency. Why do I invest mainly in crypto and blockchain related assets? Because I truly believe they are one of the biggest revolutions undergoing in this very moment and that this is the perfect time to get involved before the market explodes to the upside and prices rise at major stocks level.

Another reason that I like cryptocurrencies and their market is that they are extremely volatile and provide the average Joe the possibility to make serious money without investing a lot. It is not a secret, in fact, that every time the market starts to rise, people rush into the search for the "next big win" and the question that circulates is always the same: "What will be the next cryptocurrency that will go to 'the moon'?"

The issue with cryptocurrencies is that being a market that is not yet regulated in several countries, the risk of pumps and dumps, manipulation and fraud are just around the corner. This is why I wanted to cover them in this book. In fact, since they provide a great opportunity, I am worried that a lot of people may get involved without knowing what they are doing and will lose a lot of money down the line. Here I want to show you what I do before investing in a particular asset and how I keep it a sustainable source of passive income.

Before getting started, here is a list of useful tools for the analysis of cryptocurrencies:

- Coincheckup.com - one of my favorite sites, offers much more data than other cryptocurrency monitoring sites;
- Coinmarketcap.com - one of the oldest crypto price tracking sites, far more popular than Coincheckup, but offers less data;
- Blockfolio - another popular cryptocurrency tracker.

Now let's get to the good stuff.

Step 1 - Understanding your risk profile

Many people will advise you to buy "low capitalization" cryptocurrencies and tokens (i.e., between 10 and 100 million dollars) because they have a greater opportunity for growth in terms of percentage.

Although this statement is relatively correct, you have to keep in mind that the smaller a coin is, the riskier it is to invest in it. Why? Because the project has indeed a much higher risk of failing.

In traditional investments, most people aim and are happy to get an annual return of 3% — 4%; but they could be in serious financial difficulty if the invested capital is lost, so most of the time more well-known, safer and more stable titles are selected.

Other people would instead be satisfied only with an annual yield of 7% — 12%. These people could also be willing to lose all their investment if things go wrong. In their case, they would point to a higher risk given the economic attitude they have at the base.

These two different groups of people have different "risk profiles".

It is important that in any purchase you make in your life (even for something "concrete" like a car), you do so knowingly about the financial risk profile you can afford to take.

My personal opinion is that just because something has higher chances of performance does not mean it is the best choice. In particular, I have invested mainly in the top 5 coins in terms of capitalization, because they are the safest spot right now. However, I always allocate a small part of my portfolio, 10% to be precise, to low cap coins. How do I find the most promising one? Here is what I do.

Step 2 - Identification of new coins or tokens

There are three main ways I usually use to find the "new" coins or tokens:

1. Through the posts of the Bitcointalk.org forum, more precisely in the section "Announcements (Altcoins)";
2. In the subreddit / r / cryptocurrency;
3. In the "Newly Added" sections of Coincheckup and "Recently Added" by Coinmarketcap.

Each of these is a great resource to discover interesting coins with great return potential over a shorter period of time. As already said, I only put in a maximum 10% of my capital into these under-rated projects.

With every investment comes the possibility to get scammed and in the crypto world it happens more often than I would like to see. During the last three years of experience, I have developed a series of principles that I follow in order to avoid being scammed. Here is what will make me decide NOT to invest in an asset.

Step 3 - Exclusion of coins and useless tokens/scams

One of the first things I do when I look at new projects is to subject them to very strict criteria to remove "fluff" projects from the list. In particular:

- I do not buy cryptocurrencies in industries and sectors that I do not understand;
- I do not buy cryptocurrencies whose teams are inactive in social media communication;
- I do not buy cryptocurrencies whose start-ups/associations/companies are registered in countries where I cannot validate a solid corporate entity;
- I do not buy cryptocurrencies if I cannot find the team members (with particular attention to the founder) on LinkedIn and validate that they are real profiles;
- I do not buy cryptocurrencies whose teams adopt spamming strategies and do aggressive and non-informative marketing campaigns on social and non-social channels;
- If a team is building a brand-new technology, I do not buy the cryptocurrency/token unless there is a detailed technical document explaining how it works;
- If a cryptocurrency has a pre-ICO with a discount, I tend not to buy it. If I did, it would only be in the case where the discount compared to the public ICO is minimal and the amount purchased is "locked" for a significant period of time (to avoid massive dumps after the public ICO);
- I do not buy cryptocurrencies if I do not use them personally as an end user.

To help me with the process, I also use a series of questions that allow me to get more in depth and realize the true fundamental value of an asset. In particular, I really like to ask myself the following questions:

- Would I use this cryptocurrency as an end user?
- Would I pay that price as a user?
- Does this project require the development of new technology?
- What is the team's experience in this determined direction? Have they already managed a successful company? What was the performance of this company?
- Does the team have the ability to develop this technology? Are engineers and developers recognized in this sector? Do they have product managers and customer support?
- Is it clear how the project will generate users/customers?
- Why are they using the blockchain? Do they really need it or do they use the term "blockchain" to hype their project up? What are the pros and cons of using the blockchain in this case and why should the blockchain improve the current alternative on the market? (Keep in mind that currently, in most cases, blockchain-based systems are slow and expensive).

Pay attention to absolutist statements. Each project has negative aspects and consequences. A real project will be realistic in delineating them, especially the latter.

If I can see that each question has a positive answer, I will then allocate a part of my portfolio. I always invest long term, and I am willing to stay in a coin for at least one year. If, for any reason, I do not feel confident enough to put money into a project for at least

52 weeks then that means that it is probably better to look at another one.

Predicting the next currency that will make the boom is impossible. There are so many projects that are based on nothing but still capitalize tens of billions of dollars. In the same way, there are dozens of serious projects that deserve more, but fail to stand out and gain visibility compared to others. The golden rule is the same as in every financial market: diversify. By diversifying between several coins, you reduce the risk.

My final tip on cryptocurrency investing is to always include Bitcoin, Litecoin, Ethereum and Bitcoin Cash in your portfolio, since those are the most supported coins by institutional investors. How do I buy those coins? Everything starts on Coinbase.

7

DROPSHIPPING – SIDE HUSTLE IDEA #3

WE HAVE COME TO ONE OF MY FAVORITE ONLINE BUSINESS MODELS. Dropshipping is a retail model where the store does not hold a stock of products but only buys them after the purchase from the client has already happened.

The supplier - typically a wholesaler or a manufacturer - receives the order and takes care of the shipment to the final customer, without specifying his identity. In the eyes of the customer, the entire transaction is managed by the store that does not actually even see the product that is sold.

To better understand how it works, let's take a concrete example.

Suppose that amazinglamps.com is an online store specializing in — guess what — lamps, which operates using dropshipping with a wholesaler in the sector. When Mr. Brown decides to buy a lamp for his daughter's wedding, does a search on Google and finds a perfect lamp for her house.

This is exactly what happens, step by step.

Step 1 - Mr.Brown places an order on amazinglamps.com

Once he chose his lamp, Mr.Brown completes the purchase by making a payment of $80 with a credit card and indicating his shipping address. The payment is deposited in the account of amazinglamps.com and Mr.Brown receives an automatic confirmation email.

Step 2 - amazinglamps.com passes the order to its supplier

Together with the confirmation email addressed to Mr.Brown, the e-commerce platform of amazinglamps.com automatically sends an email to the supplier with all the order details including the item code ordered and the shipping address.

Amazinglamps.com has already left a credit card to its supplier to use for each order. The supplier, therefore, uses this card by withdrawing an amount of $50, or the cost of the lamp according to the price list reserved for amazinglamps.com.

Step 3 - The supplier sends the lamp to Mr.Brown

The supplier sends the ordered article to Mr.Brown, using a package with the amazinglamps.com logo. Once the order has been sent, the supplier sends a confirmation email to amazinglamps.com, including the $50 invoice and the tracking number for tracking the shipment on the shipper's website.

Step 4 - amazinglamps.com warns Mr.Brown of the shipment

Once the shipping confirmation has been received from the supplier, the manager of amazinglamps.com uses its e-commerce platform to send a confirmation email to Mr.Brown.

The email also contains the tracking number and a link to the shipper's website that Mr.Brown can use to track the position of his package in real time.

Step 5, the big step - Mr.Brown receives his lamp and happily gifts it to his daughter

After a couple of days, Mr.Brown receives the package of amazinglamps.com and shows satisfied his purchase to his wife, who finds the lamp very elegant. The following week, Mr.Brown gifts the lamp to his daughter.

Despite its fundamental role, throughout the transaction, the supplier is completely invisible to Mr.Brown. On the package, there is the logo of amazinglamps.com, and there is never any reference to those involved in packaging and shipping the package.

In fact, the wholesaler is as if it did not exist for the final customer. His sole responsibility is to store the products and send them when an order is received. Everything else - development and management of the e-commerce site, marketing activities, customer service, etc. - is the responsibility of the retailer.

This model is often referred to as the ultimate solution for those who want to start an online business. Without a doubt, it is the simplest model but in fact, has its pros and cons that I want to show you one by one.

Benefits

Minimum investment - Probably the biggest advantage of dropshipping is the possibility of launching an e-commerce store without having to invest thousands of dollars for the purchase of products. With the dropshipping model, in fact, you do not have to buy any product until the moment you have already sold it, and you have already received payment from your customer. It is, therefore, possible to start a successful dropshipping business with an investment close to zero.

Easy to get started - Carrying out an e-commerce business is much easier when you are not dealing with physical products. With dropshipping you do not have to worry about:

- Managing or paying for a warehouse;
- Packing and shipping your orders;
- Keeping track of inventory;
- Managing returns;
- Managing stock reorders.

Reduced expenses - Not having to deal with the advance purchase of products in the catalog or with the management of the warehouse, your expenses are very low. You can safely run a dropshipping business from home with your laptop, spending less than $50 a month for your Shopify store plus some useful accounting tool.

As your business grows, your expenses also increase, but they will always be very low compared to those who run traditional e-commerce (or even physical) store.

Independence from the workplace - A dropshipping business can be managed from anywhere in the world as long as there is an Internet connection. All you need to do is update your site, communicate with customers and pass orders by email to suppliers. If you think about it, this aspect is very important and can literally change your life.

You will probably never work lying in a hammock on a tropical island, but the fact that you can do it will make you feel better. If nothing else, you can choose your usual place of work, away from the chaos and traffic and this will make your routine much better.

A wide range of products - Not having to buy the products you sell in advance, means that you can add to your catalog all the products that suppliers provide you with. If a product is in stock, you can sell it on your e-commerce site at no additional cost. Despite this is a great advantage, you have to be careful not to get too caught up, putting up an online superstore that sells everything. Most people prefer niche stores rather than larger ones.

Even with dropshipping, it is essential to select a specific niche that gives your business a clear and well-defined shape.

Scalability - With a traditional business, if you receive double orders, you typically have to work twice as hard to sort them out. With dropshipping, however, most of the work is done by your suppliers allowing you to grow without weighing on your shoulders too much. Especially if your processes are automated, you will actually have an increase in work only for customer service.

On Shopify there is a very popular app that allows you to put the autopilot to your online store, taking care of sorting the orders in real time to one or more of your suppliers based on the products sold.

All these benefits make dropshipping a very attractive model for both beginners and experienced traders. Unfortunately, it's not all sunshine and rainbows.

All this convenience and flexibility has a price to pay.

Disadvantages

Low margins - The main problem with dropshipping is the low margins per order that can usually be obtained. This is because buying a product only after selling it; you cannot use the same price lists that are reserved for those who buy large volumes in advance. As a result, to remain competitive and not go off-market with the selling price, you have no choice but to keep your top-ups low.

As we have seen, the perfect product to sell online has a surcharge of 500% compared to the purchase price. With dropshipping, you can forget about a margin of this kind, and you can expect to reach 30-40% at the most.

To mitigate this problem, you can always deal with your suppliers when your sales become regular and your orders, even if diluted over time, start to have important numbers. However, this will not happen in the first few months of your business, so you'll have to consider fairly tight initial earnings.

Problems with products availability - If you manage your products, it is relatively easy to track the availability of what you are selling. If on the contrary, you supply from one or more wholesalers who distribute your products to other merchants, the availability can vary very quickly within a day.

In theory, you could solve this problem by integrating with your suppliers' warehouse software, but this is not always a viable path, also because the technological equipment of your suppliers may not be as evolved as you would like.

Complex shipping costs - If you work with more than one supplier, you may have products in the same order that will be shipped from different warehouses, multiplying shipping costs.

For example, if your customer enters an order with two products belonging to two different wholesalers, two parcels must be shipped, and shipping costs will be double. To offer a quality service, you will have to pay for these additional expenses resulting in a loss on your profit margin.

Vendor errors - Have you ever been accused of something that you did not have any fault but that fell under your responsibility?

Even the best suppliers make mistakes, and when it happens, you'll have to take on all the responsibilities and apologize to your customer. Remember that in his eyes there is only your store and as well as giving you positive feedback in the case of a good shopping experience, he will complain to you in case of problems with his order.

The question at this point is whether, considering all these disadvantages, it is worth adopting dropshipping as a business model.

As I said at the beginning, it is not a perfect model and although it has indisputable advantages it also brings with it the problems you need to consider and be able to deal with.

The good news is that with little tricks and proper attention, many of these problems can be mitigated and will not prevent you from setting up a profitable and long-lasting business.

To understand how to do this, you need to analyze what the players are doing in a dropshipping distribution chain and their roles in the order management process. Once you have a clear picture of the situation, you will have all the elements to start moving and designing the structure of your new online business.

How a dropshipping distribution chain works

The term "supply chain" is used to describe the entire path of a product that goes from its concept to delivery in the hands of the final customer.

For the purposes of this guide, there is no need to go too far beyond this definition. The topic is very complex, and ten chapters like this would not suffice to treat it with an appropriate level of detail.

What you need is to understand which are the 3 main players that form a distribution chain, i.e., who are the producers, wholesalers, and retailers and what is their function in a dropshipping sales system.

Producers - Producers create the product and, instead of selling directly to retail, supply wholesalers or retailers who regularly feed their business with large volumes of orders.

Buying directly from the manufacturer is undoubtedly the cheapest way to get your product, but very often the manufacturers do not accept individual orders and do not take care of storage and shipping. For these reasons, they are generally not very suitable suppliers for a dropshipping model, and it is more convenient to contact wholesalers.

Wholesalers - Wholesalers buy products in large quantities from manufacturers, apply a top-up and resell them to retail stores. Very often they are specialized in a particular niche of products and do not sell directly to the public.

Retailers - A retailer sells directly to the end customer, buying from wholesalers or sometimes from manufacturers and applying their own margin on the selling price. It is at this point in the distribution chain that the product comes into contact with potential buyers and must be good enough to convince the consumer to buy it.

In the typical distribution chain, therefore, the product goes from the manufacturer to the wholesaler and from the wholesaler to the retailer. During the journey, price increases because each "ring" of the chain adds more services and applies additional mark-up. At the same time, the added value of the product also increases, in terms of marketing and customer care.

The same pair of shoes thrown on a shelf in a warehouse or displayed wisely in a shop window does not have the same commercial value. Customers do not just buy the product itself but all the shopping experience around it, and this applies to both traditional commerce and online commerce.

Your role will be precisely to select the right niche, buy products from a reliable supplier and add value through your experience and the care of your customers.

It is important to note that there is no dropshipper role in the distribution chain because dropshipping is not a role but a service that could be offered by each of the three links in the chain.

To get the best prices, you should try to address directly to wholesalers or producers, then presenting yourself as a retailer.

How to find the right wholesale suppliers for your dropshipping business

In a dropshipping business, you are tied hands and feet to your suppliers - for better or worse - and more than any other business model your supplier plays a leading role in the success or failure of your online store.

You can search for your suppliers in different ways. You can also try other methods, compare results and make your own assessments. The decision is very important, so take all the time you need.

Contact the producers

Once you have defined your market niche, contact the manufacturers directly and ask for a list of their wholesale distributors. From this list, contact the distributors one by one and ask if they offer dropshipping service. After a series of phone calls, you will begin to understand what the industry leaders are in your area and you will be able to select the ones that best suit your business.

Search on Google

When looking for dropshipping distributors on Google, there are some important rules to keep in mind:

1. Scroll through the results pages - Wholesalers are terrible in marketing and promoting their business, and you will not find them on the front page looking for "wholesale distributors for product X." This means that you will have to scroll through hundreds of search results before finding your distributor's site on page 77, or some page near the end of the results.

2. Do not judge them for the quality of their site - For the same reasons as above, do not expect to find sites with ultra-modern graphics. At best it will seem to you to jump into the past, back in the 1990s. However, this should not discourage you. Their job is to manage a warehouse of products, not to promote an online business. That's yours, by trade.

3. Modify your search - If you do not find what you are looking for, try changing the terms of your search, interchanging words like "distributor," "retailer," "wholesaler," "wholesale," "warehouse" or "supplier".

In online research, you must also be very careful with fake or untrustworthy distributors. To recognize them, you have to pay attention to those characteristics that are typical of unlawful wholesalers and that, if present, should make you ring an alarm bell.

Generally, online distributors should be avoided if one of those circumstances are in place:

1. Require a monthly subscription - Real wholesale distributors do not ask for a monthly subscription for the privilege of doing business with them. If a supplier asks you to sign up for a membership, it is likely that it is not a legitimate distributor. It is possible and quite legitimate,

however, that it requires a few dollars for the packaging costs that must be incurred for each order sent.

2. They sell to the public - A genuine distributor does not sell to the public at "wholesale prices." Before applying a dedicated price list, you want to know if you are a reseller with all the right credentials before accepting the first order. So if you find a distributor that allows you to do a dropshipping business as a private individual, it is appropriate that you ask yourself some questions about the seriousness of its service.

Make an order from the competition

If you think that an online store operating in your own niche - that is your potential competitor - uses dropshipping as a business model, try to make a small order on its site. In the package that you will receive, the shipping address for returns will be indicated and by looking for that address on Google, you will be able to trace back to its supplier and contact him.

Participate in trade shows in the sector

Trade fairs give you the opportunity to get in touch with manufacturers and suppliers operating in your own niche. Meeting them all together and talking to each other in person can be a good way to evaluate your options and present your business idea.

Use an online directory

A distributor directory is a database organized for markets, niches or products that can be very useful in finding a dropshipping supplier or in the brainstorming phase of your niche.

One of the main advantages of this strategy is that you can find thousands of distributors and millions of products in one place. The database managers have already selected distributors, so the risk of finding an illegitimate service as we have seen before is close to zero. The disadvantage is that you will probably have to pay to access the database.

If you want to go down this path, I would like to point out World-wideBrands.com, the best online directory of this type. Since 1999 it provides a serious and reliable service when it comes to data sharing.

We have seen how the selling process in dropshipping works, what are its advantages, its disadvantages and what are the possible strategies to find the right suppliers.

Although not perfect, it is undoubtedly a very interesting business model, especially for those who are beginners with online sales. In America, we are still a step behind compared to other countries and the dropshipping distribution is not very mature yet. While this is an obstacle to your business idea, it also represents an opportunity, because less spread also means less competition. The field is still fertile and starting now means taking a competitive edge that can be decisive in the future.

Once your store is up and running, it is possible to turn it into a passive stream of income. How? Once again, the best way to do it is to contact a virtual assistant. This time, his job will be to send the orders to the wholesalers you are working with and making sure that the details are properly transmitted. When you are earning enough to pay someone to take care of this process, which normally costs around $60 per month, you can then focus on scaling the business or enjoying the profits you are making.

8

SELF PUBLISHING – SIDE HUSTLE IDEA #4

IF YOU ARE AN ASPIRING WRITER AND WOULD YOU LIKE TO SELL YOUR first works online or just someone that likes the royalty business model, then Amazon is your best resource. If you want to distribute your books in electronic format, it is one of the best solutions you can find. It has a large audience and allows you to do everything in no time. Just think about it, you are reading a book that you bought probably on the most popular e-commerce in the world, and I leveraged this possibility to make money.

One thing that a lot of people think is the fact that there is a lot of work required in writing and publishing a book. Well, I am here to tell you that it is not as complicated as it may seem. In fact, what I personally recommend (and do) is to outsource the writing of the manuscript to a writing company or a freelance. You will be surprised to learn that you can get a high-quality book written for around 250$. What writing company do I suggest? I have had an amazing experience with E-Writers-Solutions, and I highly recommend it.

Now it is time to see how to properly publish your book on Amazon.

Following the guide I am about to propose, you can find out how to publish a book on Amazon in a totally free way and having your book for sale at the price you want within twenty-four hours. Try it and good luck with your career as a writer!

Before seeing in detail how to publish a book on Amazon, you have to do a couple of very important operations. First of all, if you have not done it yet, you have to register on Amazon for free. It takes only a few seconds, and I assume you are already familiar with the platform.

Next, you must prepare your book for publication on Amazon trying to comply with all the parameters required for its layout (index, chapters, cover, etc.). You can find all the information you need in the official Amazon guide to prepare books in electronic format. All the most common types of digital documents are supported, but it is recommended to use the HTML format or Word DOC / DOCX.

After signing up to the site and preparing your masterpiece, you can publish a book on Amazon by visiting Amazon Kindle Direct Publishing. Then log in with your Amazon account information and complete your profile information by clicking on the Update link at the top. You will need to fill in two forms: one with your personal information (name, address and telephone number) and one with your tax information (you must clarify if you are a private individual or a company, if you are a US citizen and answer other questions that will allow you to validate your identity and proceed with the publication of the book).

After having provided Amazon with all the requested data, go back to the initial page of the Direct Publishing Service and click on the "Add a new title" button to start publishing your e-book. Then, fill out the form that is proposed to you with all the information related to your work, such as title, description, cover, genre, selling price to the public, etc. and click on the "Save and Continue" button to complete the book publishing process.

As for the economic side of the issue, the publication of books on Amazon is free and you can collect royalties for a total of 70% on the sales of the book if you choose a price between 2.99 and 9.99 dollars or 35% if prices between $0.99 and $2.00 dollars are chosen (in every market). You can also join the KDP Select program that allows you to expand the availability of the book to the international versions of Amazon and to get some money even from the loan of the work (while maintaining an exclusivity on the digital publishing of the book).

Once you have gone through the process, you will just have to wait up to a day, and then your book will be live. Most guides end here, but I want to give you some more insights on what to do to extrapolate the most amount of profits.

First of all, you should convert your e-book into paperback and audio versions. You can do this on two of Amazon's platforms: KDP and ACX. The first one allows you to publish a hard copy of your manuscript for free, using a functional print on demand service. ACX, instead, was created to allow writers to produce high-quality audiobooks, starting from their creation. You can either pay a narrator upfront (usually the price ranges from $30 to $50 per finished hour) or you can do a royalty split. If you are short on money, splitting royalties with a narrator is a great way to get that extra revenue for free, but if you want to build a huge business, like mine (I make $6,000 a month from self-publishing alone), you should definitely pay upfront to get the full benefit.

After you have created and published the audio and paperback version of your book, you can experiment with other publishing channels. My favorite ones are Draft to Digital and PublishDrive.

You can even get your book translated into different languages for free through BabelCube, always following a royalty split model.

So, to sum it up here is the process to publish a book to create a passive income stream:

1. Get the book written by E-Writer Solutions;
2. Get the book cover done on Fiverr;
3. Publish the book on Amazon KDP;
4. Publish the book on ACX, paying your narrator upfront;
5. Publish your book on Draft to Digital;
6. Publish your book on PublishDrive;
7. Translate your book through Babelcube for free.

This is the script I follow, and that makes me money on autopilot. If I could advise you on a business model, self-publishing would definitely be my choice.

9

DOMAIN FLIPPING – SIDE HUSTLE IDEAS #5

Humans have traded objects to make a profit since ancient times. Even Neanderthals exchanged polished stones for rags and vice versa trying to make money. Websites are the "big deal" of the 21st century. By now everyone can open their own site or blog on platforms like WordPress, and just as easily can sell it thanks to sites like Flippa.com.

This is one of the best business opportunities that there are online to create a passive income stream. When I talk to my students about this model, I like to explain it as "online real estate". Like in the previous chapter, where we discussed how profitable it is to buy a house to rent it out or to flip it, you can do the same thing on the internet. There are two advantages, though, that make this a much more approachable solution. First of all, the amount of capital required to invest is not as high as real estate. If you have $500 to invest in this business you are already in a great position (consider the fact that you can get started with just $100). Secondly, do not forget that using a website like Flippa gives you enormous exposure to the public and allows you to flip businesses much quicker than when dealing with physical properties.

Without further ado, let's get started!

Flippa is the number one portal for selling and buying websites: it boasts a huge audience and offers excellent tools to increase the visibility of your online auction. If you are going to commit a bit of capital, a little time and a lot of "rags," the buying and selling of sites on Flippa could bring you great profits and build, over time, a nice income stream.

The platform has sold sites for 140 million dollars since the launch in 2009. If you want to contribute to increasing this amount, you should read the following pages.

Find a niche

Before investing a single dollar, you must be clear about what your site will look like and what it will talk about. In this phase, it is good to find a niche with potential and start from that. Alternatively, if you think you have knowledge on a certain topic that can be considered a niche, then design the blog in that direction.

Focusing on a specific "small" sector is already a first step in cutting out large numbers of competitors. Obviously, the niche must have at least a little bit of a client base. You don't want to waste your efforts, right?

Building Vs. Buying

Well, you found your industry, now it's about securing a site, and then the doubt that arises is: build it, or buy it? Let's see what are the pros and cons of both cases.

1. Build your site

Unless you're a web developer, creating a site from scratch can cost you a few hundred dollars - unless you buy one already existing, anyway. You can also follow an ad hoc course, but the quickest way is definitely to hire a programmer who does the "dirty work" and build your blog on a solid foundation.

Creating it on WordPress would be good. Those who buy websites, generally, know this platform and therefore tend to buy preferably WordPress sites. Once the site is set up, you need content that is focused on keywords and full of affiliate links.

The ways to follow are essentially two: either you create all the content or pay someone to do it for you. Sites like Fiverr put you in touch with copywriters, writers, graphic designers and much more (the texts cost an average of $5 for 500 words).

When you have accumulated a lot of material, avoid publishing it all in one step and dilute it over time, following the classical one/two articles per day patter.

2. Buy your site

Very often buying a site already started will cost you more than creating it from scratch, but at the same time, you will enjoy some significant benefits. First of all, a consolidated public (more or less numerous), and according to the site will already be indexed on search engines.

The key point is to buy it for less than it actually is worth. You must be careful of at least three factors when approaching a seller of underserved sites:

- the owner does not update it very often;
- the site does not make much money;
- the owner seems disinterested in his business;

If you find something with these features, consider making an offer. But if finding the "perfect site" that meets these requirements becomes too exhausting or steals too much time, you can rely on a site broker. Many of these are commissioned and have access to huge databases of sites. Just tell them the key points, and they will find the site that's right for you.

Once you have purchased the site, use all the means you have to grow it, increase traffic and earn money.

Sell sites on Flippa

When your site has achieved good traffic, engagement and earning potential it is time to put it on auction on Flippa. Here are some suggestions for creating a successful auction.

1. Prepare a detailed description

As also reported by Flippa in a blog post, the auctions that are less successful are those with little information in the descriptions. Few data available reflect the shortage of the seller and the site itself. Possible buyers might think that if you did not want to write a description, how well could you have managed your site?

Try to write an understandable text, with a professional tone, able to generate interest and inspire security.

2. Enter the statistics

It may seem obvious, but the first thing that a possible buyer will read will be the statistics of your site. So make sure that they are as up-to-date as possible, especially with regard to page views and gross revenue.

3. Do not be anonymous

Try to imagine offering hundreds of dollars to a seller without a name, without a face or a social account. Would you rather not know who you are dealing with? Those who buy feel much safer to negotiate with a real person, especially when the price of the site is significant. Your name and your face tell the buyer that you have nothing to hide and you are not a scam artist. The first thing you need to earn is your client's trust; the second is his money.

4. Reach the "most active categories" on Flippa

If your auction is very popular, Flippa could put it in the "most active" category. This does not cost you anything, but it gives you a lot of visibility, putting you in front of thousands of buyers. The advice I've given you so far should help you get more offers, but if you realize they are less than what you expect, try the following.

Let's say you've launched an auction and you already received an offer in the early hours, as a seller you can decide whether to accept it or wait to receive more. Once you approve the first, the others will follow automatically. If you set aside more offers without approving them and then do it at once, Flippa's algorithm acknowledges that your auction is very busy. So you have more chances to finish among the "Most Active" ones.

5. Create a sustainable product

How much maintenance does your site require? How much will the buyer have to work to make it profitable? Offers may stop if buyers realize that the site needs more time than it actually is worth.

So try not to worry about them and make sure your site is sustainable, starting with the contents. Let's say that they are all flour of your lot and that have allowed you to save money. But think how the customer can react knowing that he will have to look for and hire a freelancer to create new posts.

If you have been relying on external writers right from the start, just pass them on to the new owner who will then have to deal with experienced collaborators.

6. Reach all potential buyers

Do not rely on the only offers you receive, try to be active in the search for new buyers as well. If the promotion through social media is not enough, contact directly the owners of the sites that are part of your niche. Maybe they may be interested in buying your site to increase earnings, or just to permanently eliminate competition.

Buying and selling sites on Flippa is not an activity you can do in one night, but if you invest time and energy, you can get excellent profits. Remember to buy or create a site that belongs to a profitable niche and make it grow so that it generates money. When you place the auction on Flippa make sure you take advantage of all the promotion channels and always be transparent with your potential customers.

I have always liked this business model because it allows anyone to start their little empire with little money. $100 are often enough to create a powerful website that will attract buyers on Flippa. After you have made your first profit, it is important to use it to fuel the business and create another website to sell.

Sooner than later, you will have enough capital to outsource the creation of the sites, and you will find yourself collecting money on autopilot. How can you do it? I highly recommend visiting Upwork.com, a powerful website that allows you to find hundreds, if not thousands, of virtual assistants that can be hired for cheap (most of them work for $2-3 per hour) and instruct them to post your listings on Flippa. I have done this before, and I really loved the freedom that outsourcing the listing part gave me.

If you do not want to go down the Upwork route, you can always try to find virtual assistants of Facebook groups or on other platforms. Just keep in mind that when you are not using a centralized and controlled platform, you are more likely to bump into scammers and people that do not take things as seriously as they should.

Virtual assistant aside, this is truly one of the purest forms of passive income and something that I am really passionate about.

As you can see, my passive income business models are not "click here to make money" type of solutions. Those do not exist, and I am sure you have understood it by now.

10

STOCK INVESTING – SIDE HUSTLE IDEAS #6

"Playing" in the stock exchange means investing in the stock market to make a profit from the change in the prices of shares over time.

The term play can be misleading because, when it comes to capital invested, you need the utmost seriousness and earning money by investing in the markets is not a game. It would be more correct to express oneself with the formula "investing in the stock market," rather than using the term play.

Usually, the objectives of the stock market "player" are related to the hope of making a profit. If the price of a company's shares is expected to rise, then the investor buys the stock in hopes of reselling it when the price is raised, thus gaining the difference in the purchase price and the selling price.

Playing in the stock market also involves bidding on a stock: if prices are expected to fall, you can "short" a stock by selling it at the current price and buy it back when the price has fallen, always gaining the difference. This type of transaction is made possible by

CFDs, contracts that base their value on movements in the price of shares on the market, and not on physical ownership of shares.

Let's start from the fundamentals to understand the true meaning of playing on the stock market.

"Playing on the stock exchange" is an expression that Americans have inherited form Italians.

As we will see below, however, you can play on the stock exchange even without money or with little money.

Until recently, the only way to invest in the stock market was to turn to a bank, its financial intermediaries, or invest in a fund.

But thanks to the advent of the internet, online trading has arrived and has radically changed the concept of playing online and investing.

Online trading involves investing in every type of financial instrument you can imagine: stocks, Forex, ETFs, raw materials, etc., all from the comfort of your home and without all the bureaucratic process that you have to face to buy stocks in a "traditional" way.

Thanks to brokers, financial intermediaries that allow traders and private investors like you to trade online, anyone can play on the stock exchange and easily make money with online trading quickly and immediately.

All this, thanks to CFDs, "contracts for difference".

What is leverage?

Through the use of financial leverage a person has the possibility to buy or sell financial assets for an amount higher than the capital held and, consequently, to benefit from a higher potential return than that deriving from a direct investment in the underlying and, conversely, to expose himself to the risk of very significant losses.

How does the leverage work?

Let's see how the concept of leverage works, starting from a simple case. Let's assume you have $100 available to invest in a stock. Let's assume that the gain or loss expectations are equal to 30%: if things go well, we will have $130. Otherwise, we will have $70. This is a simple speculation in which we bet on a particular event.

In case we decide to risk more for our investment, in addition to our $100, also another $900 borrowed, then the investment would take a different articulation because we use a leverage of 10 to 1 (we invest $1000 having a capital initial only of 100). If things go well and the stock goes up 30%, we will receive $1300; we return the 900 borrowed with a gain of $300 on initial capital of 100. So we get a 300% profit with a stock that only gave a 30% return. Obviously, on the $900 borrowed, we will have to pay interest, but the general principle remains valid: the leverage makes it possible to increase the possible gains.

Considering further the case of the investment in derivatives, let's assume we buy a future that, within a month, gives the right to buy 100 grams of gold at a price set today of $5,000. We could physically buy the gold with an outlay of 5000 $and keep it waiting for the price to rise and then sell it back. If we decide instead to use derivatives, we should not have $5,000, but only the capital needed to buy the derivative. Let's say that a bank sells for 100 $the derivative that allows us to buy the same 100 grams of gold in a month to $5,000. If in a month the gold is worth 5,500, we can buy it and sell it immediately, realizing a gain of $500. With the $100 of the price of the derivative, we make a profit of $400, or 400%, with $100.

This is how leverage works. Do you get the amazing power it can give to the average investor?

What are the potentials of its use?

The potential of leveraging is clear. But be careful: the leverage multiplier effect, described with the previous examples, works even if the investment goes wrong. For example, if we decide to invest $100 in our possession plus an additional sum of $900 borrowed, if the stock depreciated by 30%, we would remain with only $700 in hand; having to return the $900 borrowed plus interest and considering the $100 of our initial investment we would have a loss of over $300 on an initial capital of $100. As a percentage, the loss would, therefore, be 300% against a reduction in the value of the share of 30%.

Another element to keep in mind is that the different financial levers can be combined: in this way speculation operations are carried out using a "squared lever" with clear reflections on potential potentials.

What are the risks related to leverage?

What may appear to be an interesting tool with positive potential for the investor, on the other hand, presents risks that must, therefore, be taken into due consideration. If the financial system as a whole works with a very high leverage and financial institutions lend money to each other to multiply the possible profits, the loss of an individual investor can trigger a domino effect by infecting the entire financial market.

Banks are typically entities that operate with a more or less high degree of leverage: against a certain net capital, the total assets in which the resources are invested is generally much higher. For example, a bank with equity of $100 and leverage of 20 manages assets for $2,000. A loss of 1% of the assets involves the loss of 20% of the equity capital.

The market has been developed for the transfer of credit risk from financial intermediaries to the market. This has meant that the traditional bank model, called "originate-and-hold" (the bank that provided the loan it remains in the balance sheet until maturity), has been substituted for many operators from the "originated-to-distribute" (the intermediary selects the debtors, but then transfers the loan to others). This has the effect of a further increase in leverage. The spread of this second bank model is one of the factors that led to the crisis triggered on the sub-prime mortgage market.

Property price inflation has supported the issuance of loans and the exponential growth of the related market, allowing banks to make huge profits and, at the same time, increase leverage. But "the money machine" could not last long and in the end, many banks found themselves without sufficient capital to absorb the losses deriving from the inversion of the real estate market trend, resulting in fact in failed companies.

In the meantime, the example of the banks has spread within the financial system by spreading to all other financial institutions: leverage had prevailed, especially in the United States, generating a huge volume of risky investments that rested on a fraction infinitesimal of equity capital. We are thinking of the issue of so-called "credit default swaps" (derivative instruments used to hedge against the default risk of the debtor). Some insurance companies were heavily exposed to the real estate market, and when the latter collapsed, and the value of mortgages fell, they began to lose without having sufficient capital to absorb the losses deriving from the issue of those instruments.

In order not to risk failing and return to sufficient levels of bank capital, capital increases (not an easy task in times of crisis), the reduction of the amount of loans to businesses (granting a lower number of new loans and not renewal of those already issued) and the disposal of other liquid assets (mostly shares) can be used. The result of all this, in the period of the sub-prime crisis, was a credit freeze and a collapse of the stock market. These are the main channels through which the financial crisis has hit the real economy. Credit rationing has affected investments, and the decline in the stock market (which adds to the decline in house prices) has reduced the value of household wealth and therefore, consumption.

We know that a certain level of leverage is physiological to sustain economic growth, even if the optimal level is unknown. But history teaches us how in an increasingly globalized and interdependent economic-financial system, leverage can be a trigger for speculative bubbles. And it is in these periods that the strongest disconnect between finance and the real economy is exposed.

Technical Analysis is the study of graphs. Looking at the charts, the analyst can understand if that stock (or market) will rise or fall in a short, medium, and long term. The Fundamental Analysis instead bases its forecasts on the "fundamental factors," like news, market rumors, company acquisitions, economic crises, political events, wars, etc.

Which is better between Technical Analysis and Fundamental Analysis? The answer is simple; as always in investments, there is no better; it depends on the investor, on his way of operating in the markets, on his degree of risk, etc. In other words, there are those who are better off with one, and there are those who are better off with the other.

I personally love the Technical Analysis much more for some reasons. Let me present some of them:

- Timing: Technical Analysis offers better Timing than Fundamental Analysis. Timing is "the right time to get into a position," the ideal time to enter the market. It is, in my opinion, one of the fundamental concepts to succeed in the stock exchange. If you use the right timing, you can afford a very tight Stop Loss, so you can only lose a little. So you cut the losses and let the winnings run, the golden rule of the stock exchange. Timing is calculated by the key levels that are achieved, and with the study of the graphs, and additionally through Technical Analysis.
- Flexibility: Technical Analysis is more flexible than Fundamental Analysis since it gives us key levels (for Stop Loss and Goals) in any time-frame.
- Discount: Technical Analysis discounts the Fundamental Analysis, basic postulate of Technical Analysis. The chart already includes all the factors, all the news, all the wars, all the economic conditions, etc. As a result, if the price has risen, the fundamentals will be bullish. If the price has dropped, the fundamentals will be bearish. I can only take care of the chart, thus eliminating many variables.

In addition to this, Fundamental Analysis has the defect that certain news is difficult to find for a common investor, and sometimes when this news arrives, it is now useless, because someone smarter than us have already used them and bought (or sold) before us.

We close with a sort of "metropolitan legend" of trading, a widespread belief (but wrong) that many still have today. Many investors believe that the Technical Analysis serves to make investments in the short term and that the Fundamental Analysis serves to make long-term investments. This is not true. Both can be used to operate in the short, medium, and long term.

So many investors will continue to appreciate one and many to appreciate the other. A good idea, sometimes, is to use both, thus combining the advantages of one with the advantages of the other. An application of this concept has been explained regarding refuge currencies and high-yield currencies in Forex.

Can technical and fundamental analysis co-exist?

Although technical and fundamental analysis are considered as opposite poles, many market participants have made a winning combination. For example, some fundamental analysts use the tools of technical analysis to identify the best times to enter the market.

Nevertheless, many technical analysts exploit economic fundamentals to support technical signals. For example, if a technical pattern on the chart indicates the possibility of selling, we can refer to the fundamental data to obtain a confirmation of this pattern.

A mix of technical and fundamental analysis is not well received by the "extremists" of both schools of thought, but the benefit we can derive from fully understanding the technical and fundamental analyst's mindset is undeniable.

11

DAY TRADING – SIDE HUSTLE IDEAS #7

IN THIS CHAPTER, WE WILL SHOW YOU ALL THE STEPS YOU NEED TO take to invest in forex from home. We will show you how to play on the forex market, how to choose the best pairs to invest in, but above all how to invest in forex and currencies.

Also, we will mention the possible methods to invest in online forex exchanges thanks to online trading. All the concepts that you will find in this guide have been written to be understood by people unrelated to the world of online trading and the stock exchange, who have decided to inquire about starting to invest in the stock market.

Investing in the forex market means buying and selling currencies, aiming to earn between the price difference (purchase and sale). In the world of the forex exchange, as in other major financial markets (for example, stock market and CFD), you can earn both when there is an increase in the value of a stock, and when there is a fall in the value of a stock.

Today, thanks to online trading, it is possible to invest in forex, simply from home, without problems. This is possible thanks to online trading platforms, better known as brokers.

Today it is possible to invest in the forex exchange mainly through the following methods:

- forex market;
- binary options trading;
- CFD trading (contract for difference)

In this case, you can choose one of the following online, regulated, and authorized trading platforms:

- Markets.com
- 24Option.com
- iqoption.com
- BDSwiss.com

In short, with online trading, everyone can start making money on the forex market. It does not matter whether you are a novice trader or an experienced trader. Online trading is offered to everyone, thanks to the training offered by its broker, which teaches the basics of trading. Moreover, many brokers today allow you to practice with a demo account, thanks to which all traders can test not only the trading platform, but they can start experimenting with their trading strategies and take their first steps in this fantastic world.

Earning more means being paid more. We usually think that others should pay us more if we want to make more money. But this is not always true: we can earn more even if we pay ourselves more, and not the others.

This is a fundamental principle underlying the financial success, first disclosed in 1926 by George Samuel Clason through his book entitled *The Richest Man in Babylon*, a great motivational classic.

The principle states that part of what you earn must be maintained. Putting aside at least 10% of what you earn - and making that money inaccessible to ordinary expenses and possibly even extraordinary expenses - you can increase this amount exponentially over time. Considering any investments, thanks to the power of the compound investment, the amount saved/invested - over the years - can become important. Many people can earn more and build their assets by paying themselves first. It is a true and effective principle today as it was in 1926.

As this 10% formula is easy, people are unwilling to listen to it and apply it. This is because you are usually looking for tricks to get rich quickly, and you do not have a medium to long-term vision. On the other hand, having a long-term investment plan is a solid foundation on which to build one's economic stability. And you can start earning more by paying yourself first from today. The earlier you start, the quicker you will build your financial success.

Using the power of compound interest

To earn more, you can take advantage of the compound interest. Here's how it works: if you invest 1,000 euros at a 5% interest, you will earn 50 euros of interest, and at the end of the first year, you will have a total investment of 1,050 euros. If you leave both the initial investment and the interest earned on the current account, you will receive a 5% interest the following year over $1,050, or $52.50. In the third year, you will earn 5% out of $1.102.50, and so on. At this rate, within 15-30 years, your money will turn into an amount well above the sum invested initially. But precisely how much does the invested capital grow? The Italian mathematician Luca Pacioli explained it in the fifteenth century: any capital doubles in several years equal to 72 divided by the interest rate.

Returning to our example: if the interest is at 5% per year, we divide 72 by 5; which makes 14.4, i.e., in 14 years and four months the initial capital doubles. The sooner you start the bigger the result will be, as you will have more time for the interest you capitalize to produce its powerful magic. Start now to save and invest for your future, even if you do not have a large sum. You do not need to have an extra sum of money. You can start with any amount and grow it over time.

The secret of paying yourself first

If you want to earn more money by paying yourself first, you have to make savings and investment a central part of your financial management, just like the mortgage payment. Get accustomed to saving a fixed percentage (at least 10%) of your monthly income and investing it in special savings account that you decide not to touch. Ideally, this step would be automatic, such as a fixed monthly deduction on your paycheck. The automation will ensure that you will not have to rely on your self-discipline, and your ability to save will not be affected by your mood, from domestic emergencies or otherwise. Continue to increase that account until you have saved enough to invest the sum accumulated in bonds, in a mutual fund or real estate (spending money on rent without building any assets is a waste). Let your investments build your assets over time, and try to live with what remains after you have paid yourself. If you want to spend, try to earn more to afford it. But never put your hands on your savings to finance a more ambitious lifestyle. The ideal would be for your investments to grow to the point where you could live with interest, if necessary. Only then will you be financially autonomous and free.

If you want to earn more, you need to create assets, not liabilities. Rather than spending all the money you earn, by enriching someone else, invest in assets that produce other income (stocks, bonds, real estate, gold, etc.). Then when your money starts to grow, educate yourself further about the best way to invest your money. Stay informed about news about investment opportunities and remember to protect what is yours through a good insurance policy. Do not blindly trust who will manage your money, but always try to improve your financial education. This will make you a financially prepared person, ready to get rich. Once you understand this, the money will follow.

What is compound interest? Not everyone may know how to respond immediately to this question. If everyone knows what the simple interest is, i.e., the one that withdraws at the end of the agreed time unit, fewer are those who know what the compound interest is, how it works and, most importantly, how to take advantage of it.

The example of a bank account is enlightening.

If on 1 January I have a net rate of 1% on my account, at the end of the year I have 101 euros. The extra euro is added to the capital and, if the conditions do not change, at the end of the second year I will not have 102 euros, but 102 euros and 1 cent where the cent represents 1% of the euro accumulated after the first year.

So far, everything is clear, but most of us cannot calculate the compound interest of an investment and tend to treat it as simple interest. This is due to its slow start, that, especially with small capital, tend to be treated as "irrelevant". However, there is nothing more wrong that an investor could do.

If, for example, after five years of investment, my capital of 100 euros is now 140, we are led to believe that the interest was 8% per year.

This is incorrect because, in doing so, we do not take into account that at the end of each period, the interest accumulated has gone to increase capital. If the interest had been 8%, composing the five years, we would have had

Initial capital: 100

- 1st year: 108
- 2nd year: 116.64
- 3rd year: 125.97
- 4th year: 136.04
- 5th year: 146.93

The difference (6.93 euros) represents almost 7% of the total.

The math behind compound interest: an easy example

Suppose we have an initial capital of 1,000 euros. The capital yields a Y% interest, and this interest is calculated on an annual basis.

What will be the value of the investment after X years?

The calculation formula is as follows:

(1) $IV = CP (1 + Y) \wedge X$

IV is the value of the investment after X years, while CP is the initial capital. Y is expressed as a percentage, i.e., 0.04 indicates 4%. The symbol $\wedge$ is the symbol of elevation to power.

The inverse calculation tends to find the Y interest of an investment that now (net of inflation) is worth IV against a CP capital invested X periods (years) ago. The formula is:

(2) $Y = (IV / CP) \wedge (1 / X) - 1$

Suppose that, after inflation, 1,000 euros invested five years ago are now worth 1,400 euros, you immediately have that the yield was 6.96%.

Let's take a look at another example

Marie has just taken the salary and can finally buy the air conditioner she needs.

But her friend Julie calls her to tell her that she has an urgent need that she cannot cope with immediately and asks her to borrow $1,000.

Marie is undecided because this would mean waiting another month before she can make her purchase.

To resolve the issue, the two girls agree on the loan provided that Julie returns the money to Mary with a 5% interest (the numbers are purely random for the example).

In this way, Marie has a greater incentive to have to delay her purchase.

When Julie returns the sum loaned, she will receive $1,050 instead of $1,000.

The following month Marie can then buy the air conditioner and, to celebrate, use the $50 interest to go out to dinner with her boyfriend.

In short, in the end, this recognition for the delayed use was not bad!

Now that we understand the concept behind the rate of interest, it is good to enter a little more in detail and make some distinctions.

In this regard, we can divide the interest rate into two broad categories:

1. The simple interest;
2. The compound interest.

Simple Interest

Let's go back to the previous example.

At the end of the period, Julie returns the money plus the interest to Mary. Soon after, however, the girl asks the same amount again to buy a new refrigerator, as the old one suddenly broke.

Marie agrees to lend the money back to her friend.

The following month Julie firmed up her debt plus new interests, again for a total of $1,050.

Now Marie is with her initial capital, plus $100 in interest, for a total of $1,100.

Interest is defined as simple when, once it has matured on the underlying capital, it does not generate further interest.

In our example, we note that the first $50 was not added to the capital loaned the second time.

Compound Interest

Change of scenery.

Julie asks Marie to lend her $1,000 with the promise to return them in two years.

Mary agrees, as long as Julie accepts a compound interest on the mature borrowed capital.

In this case, Julie will not have to pay the interest immediately at the end of the 1st year but will add the $50 interest in the capital, which in turn will accumulate 5% in the 2nd year.

At the end of the agreed period, Julie must therefore return:

- $1,000 capital

- $50 interest for the first year ($1,000 + 5%)
- $52.50 interest for the 2nd year ($1.050 + 5%)

The total capital to be returned to Mary is, therefore, $1,102.50.

Here we have materialized $2.50 more than the previous example, due to the compound interest.

The interest is defined as compound when, once it has matured on the underlying capital, it is added to the latter and contributes to generating further increased interest in the future.

Do you understand why the compound interest is your new best friend?

When you deposit your money in the bank account you are doing as Marie, that is, you are "lending" your money to the bank, which uses them to perform its credit function and lend it to people and businesses.

As a reward for this service, you are given an interest in the sums deposited, that is, a reward for the fact that you delay their use.

How to take advantage of the compound interest

If you do not want inflation to eat a nice slice of the real value and the purchasing power of your money, you have to make sure that the latter accrue compound interest over time.

Certainly, a part of the liquidity at your disposal you can deposit on one or more deposit accounts, or accounts with limited operations, where higher interest rates are recognized.

For example, you could deposit your emergency fund.

The rest, however, you should invest in a portfolio of efficient financial instruments that protect your capital and create added value.

The compound interest must, therefore, be exploited for at least two reasons:

1. Increase savings while waiting for their use;
2. Defense against inflation.

A wise thing to do is, therefore, exploit the power of compound interest to make the value of your money grow faster, protecting it from loss of purchasing power.

Try to keep only small amounts on bank accounts that give you little to nothing.

You can leave just the right liquidity for your daily expenses and the emergency fund.

Here are seven things to keep in mind.

1. Plan the investment

The first advice that we can give you about financial investments is about the planning of investments, or understand what the best actions to buy and diversify your portfolio are.

Even if you have never experienced this chain of events first hand, it's not a problem. Sooner or later, you have to learn.

To better diversify your currency portfolio and understand where to invest, we recommend opening a demo account.

The demo account allows you not only to plan investments but also to:

- Carefully analyze the stock market on which you want to invest;
- Plan your investment strategies;
- Familiarize yourself with the platform;

- Get familiar with the market.

If you decide to buy shares unconsciously and then open a real account and invest without the right measure, then prepare to say goodbye to your immense capital.

Of course, this is not the most appropriate and wise way to invest.

2. Draw the investment plan you just made

To quote W. Edwards Deming, world-renowned essayist and quality-management consultant:

> "If you cannot describe the process of what you're doing, you do not know what you're doing."

As for everything that requires a certain discipline, it is important to outline its investment strategy: in this way, it will be easier to articulate it. Once your strategy is written, look at it to make sure it meets your long-term investment goals.

Writing and schematizing your strategy will give you a firm base to start again in times of chaos and will make you avoid making important trading decisions dictated by emotionality.

It offers you a clear outline to review and change if with time and experience, you will notice defects or if you change your investment goals.

If you are a professional investor, having a written strategy in black and white will help your clients better understand the investment process you are proposing.

3. Learn the difference between investing and speculating

Understanding the difference between a trader and a speculator is very important. You need to know how to "use" the difference if you want to make the most out of your investments.

Before buying currencies, you have to evaluate:

- what do you want to get from the markets;
- what is your level of risk tolerance;
- if you are investing;
- if your goal is to speculate on the markets;
- the time you have available to spend on investments.

If you want to get the maximum profit in a tight time, then you must have a considerable time to devote to the study of markets and financial instruments. So you must understand the difference between speculator and investor.

What does a speculator do?

The speculator is that trader who buys and sells shares to make a profit in the short term; in this case, we are talking about very narrow trade times ranging from a few minutes to a few weeks.

We do not talk about years or months.

They only take advantage of the price difference between the value of the sale and purchase of the deal.

The speculator's characteristic is that it is not interested in dividends distributed by listed companies.

What does a trader do?

Contrary to the previous one, the investor also defined as a long-term investor, invests his capital by providing liquidity to the currency pair.

In this case, the trader will buy the so-called "lots" of a given currency. The goal of a trader is to keep the stocks in his wallet for a prolonged period and turn them into profit!

This allows him to benefit from the detachment of the dividend that is added to the possible appreciation of the title.

Very important in this case is to understand what kind of investor you are. Pay close attention to this step because it is essential to earn with investments in the forex market. Most of the trader's operating strategies are based on fundamental analysis that is very different from those of a short-term investor or speculator.

4. Understand the importance of timing (and the impossibility of getting it right)

Very important is to understand when is the right time to buy and sell currencies.

In this case, the timing is an indispensable part to identify the stocks to be bought.

If the correct price levels are not identified, there could very well be the risk of entering the market at a risky point.

This could be unfavorable and does not allow us to quantify the transaction's risk-return ratio accurately.

5. Learn your strength and weaknesses

Does your investment strategy follow your idea of how investments depreciate or appreciate? If so, how do you exploit your knowledge?

This question refers to your actual knowledge of the market. Ask yourself: "What makes me smarter than the market? What is my competitive advantage?"

You may have special knowledge of the industry or have access to a study that few others know.

Or, you could get your own opinion by exploiting some market anomalies, as happens in the strategies for the purchase of securities with a low price/value ratio.

Once you have decided what your competitive advantage is, you need to decide how you can use it profitably to develop a trading plan.

Your investment plan should include rules for both purchase orders and sales orders. Also, keep in mind that competitive advantage could lose its profitability and its effectiveness if other investors begin to adopt your investment strategy.

Or, you can be convinced that markets are efficient, which means that no investor will ever have a real competitive advantage.

In this case, it is better to focus on minimizing commissions and transaction costs by investing in passive instruments such as futures.

6. Is your strategy versatile?

There is an old way of saying on Wall Street:

"The market can remain irrational longer than you can remain solvent."

Successful investors know where their investment performance comes from and can explain the strengths and weaknesses of their strategy.

As trends and economic issues change, many investment strategies have periods of great performance followed by periods of poor performance.

Having a good understanding of the weaknesses of your investment strategy is essential for maintaining confidence in the market and investing with conviction, even if the strategy is temporarily "out of fashion".

7. Understand that a good strategy can be measured

It is difficult to improve or fully understand something that cannot be measured.

For this reason, you should always have a benchmark to measure the effectiveness of the investment strategy you are using.

This benchmark must be consistent with investment objectives, which in turn must tune into your strategy.

There are two types: the relative benchmark and the absolute benchmark. An example of a relative benchmark could be the EURUSD pair. An example of an absolute benchmark could be a performance target.

Even if it is a time-consuming process, it is important to consider the amount of risk you are taking concerning the investment benchmark. This can be done by recording the volatility of portfolio returns and comparing it with the volatility of benchmark returns over a certain period.

12

USE FACEBOOK TO PROMOTE YOUR BUSINESS – SIDE HUSTLE IDEAS # 8

THE BEST CONTENT ON FACEBOOK IS THE ONE THAT INVOLVES AND stimulates communication. There is no single formula to write successful content, but there are some tricks that can help you increase the effectiveness of your posts:

- Publish posts in the best time. Analyze when your audience is online to optimize your publication time.
- Evaluate your Audience. Track the performance of your posts and find out what they like most and what is the winning content for your editorial plan. I will talk shortly about the importance of analytics.
- Take advantage of current issues and trends. Find out what are the topics that infect users using services like Google Trends, Trending Topic on social media or follow the calendar of events for your industry (even local ones, if they are relevant to you).
- Use the questions as a call to action to encourage users to leave comments under your publication.
- Miscellaneous content. The predictability of your posts can damage your strategy: try different types of content,

alternating topics, and formats of your publications not to bore your audience.

The video format is interesting not only because Facebook tends to prioritize it, but also because, among the various types of content that you can publish on your page, it is the one most loved by users.

Here is a small selection of tips for video optimization for Facebook:

Upload videos directly to Facebook because posts with YouTube links lose visibility (Facebook gives priority to videos uploaded on its platform)

Ideal format: Facebook recommends using MP4 and MOV, a complete list of recommended formats you can find Facebook recommends uploading videos with a maximum duration of 15 seconds, with attractive and high-quality content.

The public on Facebook also appreciates long read texts when they are written well (if the theme is current, it is easy to generate conversions): why shouldn't the same rule work for the video?

Upload the videos with subtitles (about 85 % of videos is shown without the sound) and do not forget to add a title and a small description to make people understand the subject of the video right away.

Video streaming is another type of content that Facebook likes so much and can get yourself a good organic reach. When you create a Live on Facebook, all your friends and followers will be notified of the start of a new stream, so everyone can follow and comment on your video live.

Content marketing and content curation are two of the words that most marketers will be interested in this year. Content marketing is a much more extensive approach that is not limited to the Facebook channel but can play a decisive role on the same platform. I speak of the choice and creation of content to be conveyed in their fan page that, if chosen accurately, with an attractive graphics and communicated in the right way (sometimes even in the right time) can become "viral" going to end even outside of our primary user target. However, by doing so, it could give us the advantage of expanding our brand positioning to other target users, who until then thought we were not interested in us. Translated into simple words: the content conveyed on the page, through sharing and "like," can attract new users to know our brand and start to follow it from the page.

Facebook insights provide much more data than before, and the service is almost similar to Google Analytics. Periodically "combing" the data helps to understand better which content is most appreciated by users and those that generate greater shares (now we can also know what are the comments with "sentiment" negative, even if the service is not very reliable). From the analysis of our pages and those of our customers, it appears that quality images (especially those released for the first time and created in house) and videos are those that reach the best level of engagement (likes, shares, comments) and consequently are more likely to spread our brand/product making it known to new users.

Once you get to the advanced level, it is important to start outsourcing your advertising campaigns so that you can focus on other parts of the business. In particular, it is fundamental to outsource the client profiling process. Here are some interesting instructions that can help you speed up the process.

To define the profile of your ideal customer, you have to remember that his position in society influences each individual. Therefore, to trace the profile of the ideal customer, we must answer questions related to these influences.

Social Influences

Cultural Systems and Subsystems

- How old is he?
- Where does he live?
- Is he a man, a woman, or both of them?
- What degree of education does he/she have? What schools did he/she attend?
- What hobbies or passions do they have?
- What are their values?
- What are their beliefs?

Social class

- What kind of work do they do?
- How much does he or she earn?

Family

- Is he or she married?
- Does he or she have children? How many?
- Does he live alone and is single?
- Does he live by his parents?

Marketing Influences

- Do they already use a product to meet the need or solve the problem?
- What kind of product do they use?
- What kind of brand?

- What features are relevant?
- What is the benefit most appreciated?
- On what price range is it oriented?
- Is the high price for the customer a way of affirming their social status?
- Do they associate high price with quality?
- What kind of advertising influences their purchase?
- Where do they usually buy?

Situational Influences

- Which environments can influence the purchase (showroom, the point of sale)?

Social Environment

- Within the group in which he/she lives and works, who else influences the choice of purchase?
- Who uses the product?
- Who pays for the product?
- Are the influencer, the consumer, and the buyer the same person?

Psychological Aspects Associated with the Product

- What are their fears?
- What problems do they want to solve?
- What consequences would it entail for an unsolved problem?
- What are the challenges they're facing?
- What are their wishes?

Emotional Aspects Related to the Choice of the Product

- What mistakes are they afraid to commit by making the wrong choice?
- What would it mean for the customer to choose the wrong product?

Now that you have answered these questions, you can trace the profile of the ideal customer.

Here's how to proceed.

Put a face to your potential client (download a photo from the internet that identifies the physical characteristics of your potential customer) and a fictitious name.

Then compile the data that will trace the characteristics of socio-demographic, psycho-graphic, and consumer experiences.

This serves to have a clear representation of him/her with whom we are going to talk and with whom we want to relate.

This exercise can lead to a great transformation to your company; in fact, it will help you understand the motivating beliefs, fears, and secret desires that influence the purchase decisions of the customer and tunes your marketing efforts and understand what solutions to offer to your market.

A great resource to boost this process and find people that met your avatar standards on Facebook is lookup-id.com. Thanks to this website, you can define your target customer through the definition of personal characteristics and get a list of people that met them.

Here is how it works.

Once you have entered the website, go on the "extract members" section. It is very easy to find on the top right of the page. From there, you want to insert the ID of a Facebook in your niche, which of course will contain people in target with your offer. The website will give you a complete and detailed list of the people in the group, which means that you have just discovered a goldmine since those will be on target for what you are offering.

On this website, you can even use the FB Search function. Once you have designed the features of your typical prospect, you can insert them in this platform to get a list of users that meet those standards. It is pretty straight forward, and it is very easy to use. Our suggestion is to play around with the website and get a grasp of its potential: once you start using it, you will never get back at the classic manual research.

Now it is time to use another great tool to make life easier and start gathering a following. First of all, install Toolkit for Facebook by PlugEx. What is this? It is an amazing tool that will allow you to do multiple actions in a matter of seconds. For instance, once you have your list and have launched Toolkit by PlugEx, you can then invite all those people to put a like on your page or to join your group.

When you start using these tools regularly, you will be amazed at how easy it is to grow your fan base and start getting significant results. One little tip that we like to give our readers is to always use a secondary account for this operation, to guarantee proper privacy protection.

A practical example

Now that we have seen how to use the two software in theory, it is time to dive into the practice and use a practical example to understand the concepts better.

So, let's say that we have a shop that sells running gear and we want to find customers that are on target with the items we sell. The first thing we want to do is to go on running groups, like this

one   https://www.facebook.com/groups/TrailAndUltraRunning/
and look for the group id. We can do that by going here https://
lookup-id.com/ and entering the previous URL. This will give us
the ID of the group. After that, we need to paste the group ID here
https://lookup-id.com/get_facebookid.php to get a list of all the
members that are inside the group.

After having done that, you can use Toolkit for Facebook by
PlugEx to quickly invite all the people on the list you just found to
leave a like on your dedicated running store page. Furthermore,
you can even invite them to your very own group, where you will
start your marketing process.

This is how you can use the two software together to boost up your
experience.

Another great thing you can outsource is the retargeting phase.
Once you have acquired a potential client, you can use an automated bot to close the sale for you. Here are some suggestions we
found very valuable.

If you're not using ManyChat, right now you're losing 60% of new
potential customers. (You're burning your money!)

Does this seem absurd?

Perhaps you do not know that Chatbots are the future of marketing. Soon we will see together what they are. For now, know that
they have incredible power; to enter people's lives like never
before.

Of course, there are e-mails, but think about it. Would anyone
open a promotional e-mail?

The truth is that some when they find them in the mailbox, they
almost automatically discard them. They have developed a natural
tendency to delete promotional emails.

They associate the email with invasive advertising. To talk to a friend, however, they use WhatsApp or Facebook Messenger.

What Do We Want to Say?

You should choose the tool to use based on your audience. If, for example, it is made up of managers, who often check e-mail, e-mail marketing may be the ideal choice.

But if perhaps, you turn to students, on average 20 years, who have much more convenience with the chat, it would be better to think of a Facebook Bot.

Do you understand what the extraordinary advantage is?

It will allow you to establish an authentic communication with your (potential or not) customer, who will open your message just like a friend. You will receive a notification on your mobile phone. You can chat with you; everything automatically.

The only thing you will have to deal with is the Bot settings.

The good news is that it is an extremely simple operation. Thanks to the services available, you will use more or less 10 minutes.

However, without knowing how to use this very powerful tool effectively, you would risk undermining this work. This is why, in this chapter, we will introduce you to the correct configuration of a Chatbot with ManyChat.

Are you ready? Let's start!

What Is ManyChat and Create a Facebook Bot in 10 Minutes

We can say that a Bot is a program that can manage, automatically and naturally, conversations in a chat with users.

It can answer questions, offer solutions to problems and make proposals, just as if it were human.

Already from this general definition, you will have guessed that you have in your hands something potentially revolutionary for you and your business. You will free your time, increasing your results.

ManyChat, What Is It?

In short, it is the simplest and most intuitive service to create a Facebook Messenger Bot.

You do not need programming knowledge. The configuration is extremely fast, and you will immediately have the opportunity to carry out a series of actions:

- Create automated message sequences.
- Send a message to all users registered in the bot.
- Use advanced tools to increase conversions.

How ManyChat Works: The 2 Basic Tools for Bot Marketing

We have just said that ManyChat is the easiest to use Messenger Marketing tool.

Despite its simplicity, however, it offers several features that make it complete and effective for your web marketing strategy.

Do you want some examples?

Automatic sequences.

This is the series of messages that, automatically, ManyChat will send to the user. You can set them as you like, based on your lead generation strategy.

Growth Tools.

Here, this is the real bomb among the tools offered. They are a series of "extensions" that add functionality to ManyChat. The most famous is the Facebook Comments Tool, which allows you to convert whoever who comments on a particular post into a member of the Bot.

(These are just some of the features you'll have available.)

Well, to make you better understand the functioning of a Chatbot; let's assume a case of real use:

The user Luke comments on the post of your product with the specific keyword that you have set. Your bot turns on and automatically sends your opt-in message; basically, a welcome message to confirm the user's interest.

Subsequently, based on the behavior of Luke, the bot will send him different messages, to achieve the goals you have set. These messages are part of an "automated sequence" that you created earlier.

The important thing is never to be intrusive - keep this in mind during the setup phase. Each time you send a message, a notification will be sent to Luke's mobile phone. This means two things:

- You will enter in his daily life;
- You will have to manage this opportunity in the best way, so as not to frustrate him (most people are not accustomed to this tool just yet, so do not overuse it).

Small and medium-sized businesses can use Facebook marketing strategies with high margins of success. In fact, with more than 2 billion active users every month, it is impossible to remove the blue social from your web marketing plan.

What Could Be the Goals of Facebook Marketing Referring to SMEs?

Brand Awareness

Facebook is a very important tool that enables small and medium-sized enterprises (SMEs) to make their products and services known, while at the same time cultivating a very direct relationship with interested users.

If on the one hand your community, made up of people who already know your products, can follow us on the blue social, on the other side it is possible to reach people who do not know us, through spontaneous sharing, or sponsored ones. The latter, through the creation of the right audience, allows us to reach new people potentially interested in our products.

Customer Care

Facebook is also one of the websites that best lend themselves to customer care, which is assistance to its customers. Indeed, given the announcement of future updates of the algorithm of the views of the News Feed, focus on customer care could also prove successful in terms of awarding the content posted.

Promotional content can still be valid, but using your social page as a place to solve problems and perplexities of its users can be key, because it can trigger conversations between friends, debates, and an engagement appreciated by Facebook algorithms.

Direct Sales

Facebook can also be used to sell your products or services. Like an e-commerce site, the platform lends itself to the possibility of direct purchase from the page, with huge benefits for users. For small and medium-sized businesses, this opportunity is an important resource for saving resources that would otherwise have to be spent on the creation and management of an entire site.

It must be said that those who do important business cannot simply rely on the social network of Zuckerberg to market their products online. Not a month passes in which the Menlo Park team doesn't release some new function for those who want to sell via the web.

How to Create a Facebook Marketing Strategy That Works?

Before starting to take action on Facebook, it is good for small and medium-sized businesses to devote time to creating a well-designed communication plan.

First of all, the goals of the strategies to be put in place must be defined.

Secondly, the public must be identified, that is the buyer, the typical customer, tracing a sort of identikit of its main characteristics such as age, place of residence, interests, level of education and more (see chapter 6 for more information about this topic).

As for the content, it will be good to dedicate only 20% of them to the promotion of your products or services so as not to tire the user with continuous offers and hype.

Finally, the tools for checking the results must not be forgotten, with the choice of the most appropriate metrics to follow to understand the effectiveness of the steps taken along the road to achieving the designated objectives. For example, if the setting up of a valid customer care campaign has been done, one of the ways to evaluate the effectiveness of the actions carried out is the analysis of the number and quality of comments received, rather than that of 'likes'.

Facebook for Small Businesses

Why should you use Facebook to market your small business?

Facebook is about to touch the ceiling of a billion users according to the latest official data released in July. The people who connect to this social network are 955 every month and 552 million every day; more than half a billion, even the number of monthly users who connect to Facebook with a mobile device - mobile phone, smartphone, tablet.

Facebook is becoming, for many, a major source of information more and more often, instead of connecting to the homepage of newspapers to see what is happening. We scroll the dashboard reading and commenting on the news linked by our friends. The 2011 CENSIS report on the American company shows that Facebook is used as a source of information by 26.8% of Americans, a percentage that grows to 61.5% in the age group of 14 to 29 years.

The quantity and nature of our relationships have been radically changed by the possibility of keeping in touch with people we do not see daily in person, but for the most diverse circumstances, we feel close. They were our friends in the past, we shared a travel experience or study, or we met online and subsequently met live.

This allows us to listen and exchange opinions, information, points of view, emotions; in this impetuous dynamic of conversations. This is an always open bar where people pass from one group to another participating in dozens of discussions. The companies suddenly find themselves "degraded" to one voice among others, which must gain attention thanks to the importance of what it says without the possibility of massively occupying the spaces of visibility. Furthermore, we must learn to speak "with" people, which means, first of all, to listen and respond.

Should your company/association/electoral committee/theater company/excitement have a presence on Facebook? In the vast majority of cases, the answer is yes. Do not fall into the trap of thinking that Facebook is exclusively the realm of lazy people; often it is a great way to "feel the pulse" of your stakeholders and can intersect with your needs and opportunities that otherwise you would not have known.

Unlike your site, where people may go once in a while, many people open Facebook every day, several times a day. If they find what you publish to be interesting enough for them to click on "like" or leave a comment, this makes you visible to their friends. Not visible in the anonymous way, like a flyer tucked in the mailbox, but with the social support of word of mouth.

An effective presence on Facebook can help you:

- Increase your visibility, spreading the posts of your blog, the videos you shoot, and the photos you take.
- Establish a more intense relationship with your customers, better knowing their needs, and obtaining important feedback on what you do.
- Motivate and gratify your "super fans."
- Promote and share initiatives, special offers, and new products.

A Facebook group is a micro-community within the largest community of the network that, focusing on specific themes, attracts people to the target.

To this, we add that the groups have recently had the blessing of Facebook after the hard blow to the business pages in the latest updates of the EdgeRank algorithm.

What happened to the Facebook algorithm?

The turning point came with the announcement of Zuckerberg

and the subsequent official confirmation on the blog of Facebook news. The Newsroom informs users of an epochal change: less visibility on the pages in favor of more personal communication and more visibility for the posts of friends and family.

Unlike pages, groups have a greater predisposition to the generation of discussions and not to the simple unilateral posting of content. Precisely this content with little interaction is the one against which Facebook wants to fight. The decision comes after the progressive descent of the engagement on the posts that over the years has characterized the Social Network of Menlo Park.

What does this mean?

It simply means that the posts on the groups will have greater visibility and the possibility to reach more easily your target audience. It seems to me, therefore, an excellent idea not to neglect them.

How to Find Facebook Groups in Target

Let us imagine, of course, that you have already identified the niche or sector on which to base your communication strategy. The first of the problems you need to solve is to find groups in which to distribute your content. I show you a couple of techniques you can use.

Facebook Searches

If you have an active Facebook account in America, you can use the search bar to find groups that meet your requirements. For example, if you look for a group that deals with social, you can write "social media" on the search bar and then apply the filter "groups" (Facebook will initially search among posts, people and so on).

If you want to get even smarter, I recommend you to use Facebook in English. You will open other very interesting possibilities! Facebook in English supports the "Graph Search," thanks to which it is possible to create more complex searches such as: "Groups joined by my friends who like social media." That is, look for groups which were added by part of my friends who like social media.

Or you might still be looking for users who like certain pages or groups in an area of interest. For example: "Friends who like Wired." You can then go to peek at the groups in which your friends have entered, going directly to their profile (privacy permitting!).

Use Facebook Tips

Of one thing we can be extremely sure of is that Facebook knows us more than we think.

It is for this reason that it will be easy for them to suggest groups that might be interesting to you based on the history of your likes and the groups in which you are already inside.

Just go to the Facebook page dedicated to groups. On the upper part of the drop-down menu, you can enter the "Discover" tab. Here you will find lots of suggestions divided by categories, including the "local" one to find geographically close groups.

This feature is available on both desktop and mobile. In the latter case, you will go to the main menu> Groups> Suggested.

I remind you that the specific features of the groups were recently incorporated into the main app of Facebook, while the app "Facebook Groups" retired in September 2017.

What to Do Before Posting Content in Groups

I already know that you're cheating to publish your content on the groups of your interest, but before starting to spam, I suggest you follow some rules.

Always look carefully at group usage policies.

Any self-respecting group manager sets up rules in their group to prevent the occurrence of phenomena such as SPAM, excesses of OT (Off Topic, i.e., ending off the arguments to which the group is dedicated), too much promotion, trolling and so on.

This means that there may be rules on the amount of content that can be submitted to the community, for example. Or that you can publish external links to Facebook only with the permission of the admin.

Policies are often indicated in the first post above, often attached with a "pin." Or they could be in the "file" section of the group. Study these rules well and behave accordingly.

Keep to general rules of good behavior.

Apart from the policies, which rightly dictate contents, times, and rhythms, there are also rules of good common life that should always be respected. If you produce content in large quantities:

1. Do not spam it all the time.
2. Always check that it is in theme with the group, that they are of quality and that they can be useful and relevant.
3. If possible, add a note to the article, a textual status that, for example, highlights a sentence of the article or that poses a question capable of generating a valuable discussion.

Remember, these are not only your contents! Subscribe to the groups, be in silent mode, and then spam your news as if there is no tomorrow, these will certainly irritate the admin and at some point they might even think to kick you out! Even more so now that the use of statistics of the group is available to the administrators.

My advice is always to balance your content with content from other sources. And it would be desirable to participate in the discussions, in addition to the normal posting!

If you already produce your content and think that it is sufficient for your strategy, it means that you skipped the previous paragraph. Read it!

For a content strategy, whether linked to the development of your business or your personal branding, you need news and content about your industry.

I know I'm repetitive, but I'll write it again: you cannot just talk about yourself! To find valid content on the web, you can use many tools like the simplest monitoring software (I think of Google Alerts or Talkwalker) or news aggregator sites like Feedly.

In the era of the so-called "content shock," where our ability to absorb information is lower than the amount of content produced, the figure of the creator becomes of primary importance. Skimming the contents and proposing the best to a community, therefore, becomes a primary role.

CONCLUSION

Thank you for making it to the end of this book. I hope it was able to provide you with all the tools you need to achieve your financial goals.

The next step is to get started with what you have learned from this book. You cannot obtain a passive income stream with a passive mentality. Getting "out there" is the first step to making anything happen and I suggest you start as soon as possible.

I hope that you find these lessons valuable and that you got the information for which you were looking. Creating a passive income lifestyle that works for you will give you an incredible feeling, especially at the beginning, when you make the first gains. I am thrilled for you to start, and I cannot wait to see your results coming in.

ALSO BY SHELDON LEONARD

BRAND IDENTITY: Building Your Breakthrough Business with Branding Pays